Catfishing

Catfishing

Complete Angler's Library®
North American Fishing Club
Minneapolis, Minnesota

Catfishing

Copyright © 1992, North American Fishing Club

Library of Congress Catalog Card Number 91-91473
ISBN 0-914697-44-7

Printed in U.S.A.
7   8   9

Contents

Catfishing's Special Situations

Acknowledgments

The North American Fishing Club would like to thank all those who have helped make this book a reality. In addition, the author would like to thank those who helped him, including:

Wife Susie, children Ryan and Elizabeth, his brother, Jim, and parents, Harry and Helen; Kentucky District Fisheries Biologist Ed Carroll; catfishermen Bob Fincher, Tim Collett, Ken Nelms, Bob Holmes, Darrell Van Vactor and Frank Billiter; and friends Don Wirth, Wade Bourne, Dave Precht, Larry Teague, Matt Vincent and Bill and Denise, and supporters Neal Hart and Earl Bentz of Javelin Boats.

Wildlife artist Virgil Beck created the cover art. Artist David Rottinghaus provided the inside illustrations. Photos, in addition to the author's, were provided by Paul DeMarchi, Maslowski Wildlife Productions, Oklahoma Department of Wildlife, Thayne Smith and Don Wirth.

And, a special thanks goes to the NAFC's publication staff for all their efforts: Publisher Mark LaBarbera, *North American Fisherman* Managing Editor Steve Pennaz, Managing Editor of Books Ron Larsen, Associate Editor of Books Colleen Ferguson and Art Director Dean Peters. Thanks also to Vice President of Product Marketing Mike Vail, Marketing Manager Cal Franklin and Marketing Project Coordinator Laura Resnik.

About The Author

Like many Americans, Chris Altman grew up catfishing. Reared on the banks of Kentucky's Big Sandy River, it was a rare evening that young Altman missed the opportunity to wet a line for cats.

After buying his first boat (a small, aluminum flat-bottom purchased with grass-mowing savings), he moved off the banks and began hunting cats in deeper waters. He ran limblines in the mornings before school; drifted creek minnows and crayfish through the holes after school; and ran trotlines and jugs on the weekends. Although his mother agonized over his long absences, Chris enjoyed his Huck-Finn boyhood. Waters were warm, and the cats plentiful; life was good.

Since those early years, Chris has used his lifelong love of the outdoors to build a career in what many outdoorsmen consider "the ultimate dream job." Chris sold his first article to *Sports Afield* in 1984 while still in college. In 1987, Chris entered the world of full-time freelance outdoor writing and his reputation in his chosen profession continues to climb.

Chris holds active memberships in the Outdoor Writers Association of America and the Southeastern Outdoor Press Association, as well as serving on the SEOPA board of directors. His articles have been published in virtually all of the major outdoor

markets. He has contributed to *North American Fisherman*, the official publication of the NAFC, as well as NAFC's Complete Angler's Library books *Freshwater Fishing Secrets* and *Smallmouth Strategies*. He now writes regularly for several outdoor magazines and is a columnist for several newspapers.

Through the years, Chris has received numerous awards from various national, state and regional organizations for his written work as well as his photographic skills.

Although Chris enjoys fishing for cats of all sizes, he holds a special fondness for big cats or, as he says, "those giants that have been haunting the depths for decades, living by their wits and outsmarting anglers. These are creatures that strike awe into those who are lucky enough to see them, and make a good heart better when they are released into the waters from which they came."

An avid proponent of catch-and-release conservation practices, Chris has caught and released dozens of cats ranging in size from 20 to 47 pounds. He has yet to break the magic 50-pound mark, but reports that he has "had him on a time or two."

Chris resides along the Big Sandy River, making his home in Pikeville, Kentucky, with his wife, Susie, their children, Ryan and Elizabeth, and a "good-for-nothing" golden retriever.

Dedication

H e was the first man to take me fishing. I can still remember clutching his shirt-tails as I slipped down the steep creek bank behind him. I remember, too, the silver-dollar-sized snapping turtle that I caught by the tail, and the haunting scream of a hawk that circled just over the tree tops. I can still feel his hands, hard and calloused, deftly showing me how to slip a worm onto a hook. And, I can vividly recall the little spotted channel cats that we pulled from the creek that hot summer day.

Now, on those occasional summer evenings when the memory of that afternoon comes to mind, I remember it as one of the finest days of my life. Catfishing, just Grandaddy and me. It was a day that would soon direct me to a lifelong avocation, and later to a vocation that certainly must be one of the world's finest.

And so I dedicate this book, with much love, admiration and appreciation, to my grandfather, Ked Lowe, a great outdoorsman who has inspired generations of other sportsmen.

Foreword

L ike many NAFC Members across North America, I was in-troduced to catfish at a very young age. It wasn't love at first sight, however. To this 12-year-old, catfish were no-fightin', bait-stealin', hand-pokin', unhookable, sons-of-guns to be avoided whenever possible. Looking back now, I know that most of my frustration was misdirected. Bullheads, or "baby catfish" to me and my young fishing partners, were the real culprits. We'd catch them by the dozen, depleting our supply of nightcrawlers in the process. That meant fewer were left for the fish we really wanted to catch, like smallmouth bass and huge carp.

As I grew older and learned more about the fish that lived in the section of the Mississippi River we haunted, the realization that catfish and bullheads were not the same fish did little to change my attitude. "Catfish" still meant lost bait and time wasted removing hooks from small, steel-grey fish that fought less than smallmouths half their size.

My beliefs were shattered one hot August night when I was 15. It wasn't that the fish we caught was so huge; no, the reason it left such an impression on me is that it almost killed my younger brother Jeff.

Jeff was about four or five at the time, barely old enough to hold my new rod and reel by himself. He could, however, cast and reel by himself, and caught a number of crappies on small minnows while the afternoon sun dipped toward the horizon. The action slowed as darkness moved in, so I began to stray from Jeff's side in an effort to relocate the school. In a matter of minutes I was a good distance down the shoreline, so I turned around and started to work my way back, not wanting to leave Jeff unsupervised near the water's edge.

Suddenly, Jeff let out a scream. I looked up to see him being dragged toward the water's edge by a powerful fish. In seconds, he would be in the fast-moving waters of the Mississippi and out of reach in the darkness. Without hesitation, I raced toward my younger brother, reaching him as his bare feet slipped into the inky waters. Grabbing the rod, I felt the powerful throb of a big fish. Knowing it had taken one of Jeff's little minnows, I figured it had to be a huge bass or possibly even a big muskie.

Finally, after 10 minutes of give and take, my partners and I were able to wrestle the struggling fish on shore. It was the biggest catfish any of us had ever seen, big enough to eat many of the carp we would catch. We didn't waste any time admiring it, however. We quickly put it on our stringer and headed home anxious to show everyone Jeff's big fish.

Things changed after that. Catfish were no longer talked about in derogatory terms, and the ones we did catch received a lot more respect than ones captured earlier. Eventually, my friends and I began to fish catfish specifically, trying everything from chicken livers to carp entrails. And we were successful, even though we never did catch one as big as Jeff's.

Now I know why catfish are one of the most popular gamefish in North America. Not only are they challenging to catch and fight like a bad-tempered bull, they are among the best tasting fish anywhere. That's one reason we asked catfishing expert Chris Altman to do *Catfishing* for our popular Complete Angler's Library book series. The other is that numerous NAFC members have mentioned that they want to learn more about finding and catching their favorite fish. In *Catfishing*, you'll learn how to locate catfish through the seasons in the types of waters you fish. You'll also learn which baits to use and when, and what tackle is best suited for the particular presentations described. You'll also learn how to target big cats, those 50- to 100-pound monsters that many anglers only dream about.

More importantly, perhaps, we hope you will gain a greater

appreciation for these much-maligned monsters. Along with the many tips on how to find and catch them, NAFC Members will learn what amazingly well-designed fish catfish really are. From the standpoint of being able to survive in environments that would kill other fish, catfish are without peers in marine life. Many feel that catfish are a primitive fish that has somehow managed to survive centuries of environmental change. Our author puts this myth to rest once and for all. And, as Altman points out, big catfish didn't get "big" by being dumb! Big cats are a big challenge for even the most experienced fishermen. That's what makes fishing for cats so much fun.

Enjoy *Catfishing*, then put in some bank or boat time and see how much your catch rates improve!

Steve Pennaz
Executive Director
North American Fishing Club

Meet The Catfish

1

An American Heritage

Catfish have reigned as king of North American waters for centuries. Long before the time of Christ, American Indians pursued these whiskered fish as a staple, a principal part of their diet. Archaeological explorations of ancient Indian villages have revealed scores of otoliths, or catfish ear bones, buried in their trash middens. Although the catfish's tasty flesh was presumably the reason Indians hunted them, their dorsal and pectoral spines were used as needles and awls. These, too, have been found in great numbers in many American Indian sites.

Indians developed many of our most effective fishing techniques. They created a bone fishing hook that is remarkably similar to what we use. Most often, these hooks were made from a deer's toe bone, although turkey bones were occasionally substituted. These hooks were often attached to long lines of hemp, hair or sinew stretched across a stream. Today, we call these "trotlines." Often, a single hook would be tied to a short piece of line and then suspended from a green, tree limb above a riverbank. Today, we call these "limblines" or "bush-hooks."

The Indians were aware of the catfish's extraordinary senses of smell and taste. One rather unique method for capturing catfish was practiced by the Choctaw tribes in what is now known as Mississippi and Alabama. They would fashion a cylindrical trap from a fresh, bloody animal hide and drop it into the water. Blood seeping into the water would attract catfish. When the angler saw a

A nice blue cat like this one is a pleasure for any catfisherman to catch. It is well worth the wait, and makes for great eating, too.

An American Heritage

fish enter the trap, he would pull a string and close the trap.

In many Southeast rivers, ancient Indians built v-shaped fish traps. Constructed out of piled rocks, so the v pointed downstream, conical fish traps were formed at the apex. Fish could then be herded downstream and forced into the traps. Today, many of these ancient rock structures are still seen in some rivers.

Europeans migrating to this country quickly discovered the catfish. It soon became one of the most desired fish in the water. Easily caught and absolutely delicious, catfish apparently appeal to every palate. By the time Samuel Langhorne Clemens, better known as Mark Twain, was born in the early 1830s, commercial catfishing in the big rivers of the South was a booming industry. Channel cats, blues and flatheads pulled from the depths of the Mississippi, Missouri and Ohio rivers were sold in local fish markets and shipped to nearby areas. Catfishing then was a respected profession.

Today, in this country, catfishing ranks second to bass fishing in angler popularity, according to a nationwide survey by the U.S. Fish and Wildlife Service. The survey found that some 14 million Americans spent some 284.5 million days fishing for catfish. Catfishing ranks fifth among NAFC Members, trailing only bass, crappies, panfish and walleyes in popularity.

Through the years, catfishing has become an American heritage, a gift passed on through the generations since long before this country was ever founded. Unlike many of our fast-paced, cast-for-cash angling activities, catfishing remains a quiet, contemplative sport whose anthem is sung by the frogs and the crickets, heralded by the coyote's howl, and accompanied by the soothing hum of a Coleman lantern. Victory celebrations are conducted on Sunday afternoons under the shade of an oak tree with enough golden fried catfish fillets, hush puppies and lemonade for all who are hungry.

Americans love catfish, and rightly so. Although they don't display the exciting acrobatics of a maddened smallmouth, catfish fight with a raw, brutal strength that would put virtually any of the more glamorous gamefish to shame. Cats are widespread, and they tend to occur in large populations. Cats feed ravenously, often providing the angler with nonstop action. Cats grow to enormous sizes, offering virtually any angler in America the chance to battle with a fish weighing more than 50 pounds—perhaps even

Complete Angler's Library

An added benefit to catfishing is the relaxation that an angler can work into a fishing session. The work begins, however, when you tie into one of those monster cats.

twice that. And, catfish flesh is not only delicious, but extremely nutritious—a perfect complement to today's health-conscious, low-fat, low-cholesterol diets.

Why, then, do American anglers misunderstand the catfish?

The Forgotten Fish

For decades, outdoor publications and writers have literally ignored the catfish. Entire magazines are devoted to other, popular gamefish like walleye, trout, muskie and crappie. You will seldom find catfish mentioned in angling literature. A typical hook-and-bullet publication might, in a good year, run one catfish article. Most, however, simply overlook the catfish angler altogether. And, when they finally spread some ink on the cat's behalf, much of it is wrong—blatantly wrong. One popular book lists all catfish as scavengers. (They're not.) Another notes that flatheads prefer stinkbaits. (They don't.) And, writers and anglers who obviously do not know that the catfish has, without question, the most highly developed sensory system of any freshwater fish, frequently label cats "primitive." Readership surveys, however, often reveal that the American angler is hungry for more catfish information.

The tackle industry, also, has ignored the catfish, as well as the catfish angler. Have you ever seen a fishing rod, reel, tackle box or boat designed specifically to meet the catfisherman's needs? Probably not. And, even when a product does indeed meet the cat angler's needs, manufacturers do not advertise it in that way. With some 14 million catfish anglers in this country, the tackle industry as a whole is overlooking—even ignoring—an enormous market.

Unfortunately, it is not just the outdoor publications and the tackle manufacturers that overlook America's catfish. Comparatively speaking, very little biological, physiological and behavioral research has been performed on these whiskered brutes. Our fisheries researchers have passed up the catfish in favor of the more glamorous species like black bass and trout. Why? Who knows. Hopefully, that will change.

The black bass is the most highly publicized fish in this country. Hundreds of books have been written about it, and the number of magazines devoted to these overgrown sunfish is staggering. Yet, with virtually nothing at all written about it, the overlooked catfish is nearly as popular as the oft-promoted largemouth. Imagine what might happen to the popularity of catfishing if something were written about it from time to time!

How To Use This Book

This book was designed to help you catch more catfish. The author scoured the country in search of America's finest catfish anglers, men and women with shad scales under their fingernails and battle scars on their hands. Voluminous piles of biological papers and research data were searched, and the most pertinent information has been included in this book for the benefit of all NAFC Members.

We will ignore those little pan-sized bullheads and focus our attention on true catfish, giant catfish—the closest thing to a sea monster that you will probably ever see.

In the next few chapters we'll introduce you to North America's big cats: the blues, channels and flatheads. We'll also provide some information on the white catfish. These chapters will reveal some of the traits apparent in each species, their habitat and environmental preferences; their behavior and migrations through the seasons, and their remarkable sensory systems. The more you know about the catfish, the better equipped you will be to catch them. Knowledge is rewarding!

We will take a look at catfish tackle, and help you select the gear you will need to battle a brute weighing perhaps 100 pounds or more. You will learn how to turn that measly little depthfinder into a remarkable catfish-finder. We will talk baits, dispel a few myths and help you select the best offerings for hungry cats.

You will learn where to find cats in rivers and streams, ponds, pay lakes and reservoirs. Also, we will reveal some of the specialized techniques of America's finest catfish anglers, as well as how to uncover catfishing hotspots. You will also discover how to catch cats while you sleep and, if you desire, how to catch big bruiser cats with your bare hands.

Try these tactics and techniques. Experiment with your own versions. Develop some new ones. Catfishing is not a static sport, but an ever-changing one. Chances are good that you will learn something new every time you hit the water.

2

America's Big Cats

nglers who fish for bass know that a smallmouth differs from its big-mouthed cousin. They spawn at different times, inhabit different realms of the water, and feed quite differently. Smallmouths and largemouths behave in distinctly different manners; they march to the beat of a different drummer. Astute bass anglers study each species individually, learning the various traits and habits, and using this information to target a specific fish. Catfish are no different. Unfortunately, the angling public still lumps channel cats in with the flatheads; the blues in with the whites. Catfish, they presume, are catfish.

Although North America's big cats look and behave similarly, they are distinctly different fish. Knowledge is the greatest, single, offensive weapon an angler can use while on the water.

With that in mind, let us take a look at America's four species of big catfish. After all, a fisherman who does not know his fish might as well be playing golf!

The Channel Catfish

The channel cat is the only American catfish with a deeply forked tail and harboring spots on its body. Its scientific name, in fact, is derived from these spots. The Greek word *Ictalurus* means "fish cat," and the Latin word *punctatus* means "spotted." Other common channel-cat names include "forks," "willow cats," "spotted cats," "chucklehead cats" and "fiddlers."

Hefting a stringer of nice cats like these can save you the cost of a workout at a gym. These four channels totaled nearly 40 pounds, and would be trophies for a lot of fishermen.

America's Big Cats

Like all other North American catfish, the channel is a member of the *Ictaluridae* family. Ictalurids possess four pairs of barbels, a fleshy adipose fin, smooth (scale-free) skin and bony spines in front of the dorsal and pectoral fins. Zoologists have discovered 37 species of Ictalurids living in North America.

The typical channel cat is olive-colored with a smattering of round, black spots. (These spots are usually absent in the very young, as well as older, larger individuals.) As channel cats age, they lose their olive tint, turning a slate blue color much like the blue catfish.

In fact, large channel cats are often mistaken for blues. The easiest way of differentiating between the two is counting the rays (bony spines) in the anal fin. A channel cat's anal fin will show 24 to 29 rays. The blue cat's longer anal fin will produce a count of 30 to 36 rays. Additionally, the lower edge of the channel cat's anal fin is quite rounded and shorter than the blue cat's, which has a straight, lower margin. The top of the channel cat's back, from the dorsal fin to the head, gently slopes and rounds slightly outward. The blue cat, on the other hand, has a distinctive, wedge-shaped back from the dorsal fin forward. Internally, the channel cat's swim bladder is divided into two chambers, while the blue cat possesses a three-chambered bladder.

During the spawning season, males typically assume a dark blue-black color and their heads become knobby and swollen while the lips thicken and look somewhat fleshy. Female channel cats have narrower heads and slimmer shoulders than males. Females also have lighter colors and more rounded bodies. As is true with most catfish, male and female channel cats grow to roughly the same size.

Like all fish, channel cats (and blues, whites and flatheads) are cold-blooded creatures (poikilothermic), with their body temperature closely relating to the surrounding water temperature. As the water temperature increases, cats become more active and feed more often. This change often dictates a change in angling tactics. The channel cat is the most adaptable of North America's big catfish. While blues, whites and flatheads have more specific environmental preferences, the channel cat is comfortable anywhere. He is more tolerant of turbidity than his cousins, and certainly is not a finicky eater.

Although they feed most often on live forage such as other

This fisherman holds what is certainly an oddity of nature. It's an albino catfish which is occasionally caught in the wild. The author has caught two in 25 years of fishing.

fish, crayfish and even insects, channel cats scavenge more often than blues or flatheads. As a consequence, they will readily take almost any bait offered to them. But, because they are basically predators, channel cats will often strike artificial lures with a flourish. Although they are most often taken with natural baits, some astute anglers fish for them exclusively with artificials during certain times of the year. Like all North American catfish, channel cats are considered nocturnal feeders, meaning they feed most actively at night.

Because the channel catfish adapts readily to his surroundings, he is the most widespread gamefish in North America. He lives in abundant numbers in the central part of the United States east of the Appalachian mountains, although stocking efforts by most game and fish departments have extended the channel cats' range to include most of the United States. Channel catfish can tolerate water temperature variations and colder water much better than blues or flatheads. In fact, some of the finest channel-cat angling on this continent is in the Canadian provinces of Manitoba and Ontario.

Most channel catfish taken by fishermen range from 1 to 10 pounds, with 2- to 4-pounders being most common. The all-tackle, world-record channel cat, as reported by the International

Game Fish Association (IGFA) and the National Fresh Water Fishing Hall of Fame (NFWFHF), is W.B. Whaley's 58-pound giant taken from South Carolina's Santee-Cooper Reservoir system on July 7, 1964. Because large channel cats resemble blue cats, it is quite possible—even quite probable—that larger specimens have been caught, but were not reported because they were assumed to be blues.

The Blue Catfish

The blue catfish is the largest North American catfish; it holds a special enchantment over catfishermen across the country. In the days of Samuel Clemens (a.k.a. Mark Twain), when commercial catfishing was a booming industry along the Mississippi River, gigantic blue cats reportedly hung like sides of beef in local fish markets. On May 14, 1854, P.R. Hoy, a naturalist who traveled through Missouri, wrote, "A lad caught on hook and line today a catfish weighing 136 pounds," from Grand River near Chillicothe, Missouri.

In 1879, the U.S. National Museum tried to obtain a large catfish taken from the Mississippi River. In November of that year, Spencer F. Baird, U.S. Commissioner of Fish and Fisheries, sent a letter to Dr. J.G.W. Steedman, chairman of the Missouri Fish Commission, asking for his assistance with the acquisition. The following quote from Dr. Steedman's reply to Professor Baird suggests catfish of that size were not uncommon: "Your letter requesting the shipment to you of a large Mississippi catfish was received this morning. Upon visiting our (fish) market this evening, I luckily found two—one of 144 pounds, the other 150 pounds. The latter I ship to you by express."

In his book, *Steamboating Sixty-five Years on Missouri's Rivers*, captain William L. Heckman mentions a blue cat weighing 315 pounds taken from the Missouri River near Morrison, Missouri, just after the Civil War. He said that at that time it was quite common to catch catfish (probably blues) weighing 125 to 200 pounds from the Missouri River.

The blue catfish is definitely a fish of the "big rivers," occurring primarily in the basins of the Mississippi, Missouri and Ohio Rivers, as well as in their major tributaries. In addition, the Tennessee River is one of the finest blue-cat fisheries in the country. Blues have been stocked in many reservoirs where they often feed

This big blue—tipping the scale at 109 pounds, 4 ounces—was a world record for George Lejewski. It was taken March 14, 1991, from the Cooper River in South Carolina.

America's Big Cats

ravenously and grow to enormous sizes. In some impoundments, however, biologists believe that these fish often fail to reproduce. Since the early 1970s, they have also been stocked successfully into several Virginia rivers. Virginia's blue-cat fishery has become one of America's premier, but overlooked, angling attractions.

Blue cats are more migratory than any other catfish. In the pre-spawn weeks of late spring and early summer, blues will migrate in large numbers upriver, often congregating in enormous schools below the dams and locks that block their run. As winter approaches, blues will often run downriver in search of warmer water. Also, blues are more pelagic than other cats, meaning they are more of an open-water fish. Blues roam widely, often in great schools, and search through the depths when foraging. Many commercial anglers report catching more blues on trotlines that are suspended under the surface than on those traditionally weighted to the bottom.

Unfortunately, America's blue catfish population has declined since 1900. Dam and lock construction along the big rivers halts the migratory runs of the blues, thus limiting their numbers in many sections of the larger rivers. By raising the water levels in many rivers, these dams also change the current flows that blue cats heavily depend upon. As our population has grown, so has the commercial harvesting of catfish. This has led to a further decline in the number of blue cats, as well as giant individuals. And, of course, the pollution in major river systems has definitely had an impact on catfish populations.

The blue cat looks much like the channel cat, although blues have a pale bluish-silver to slate-blue coloration throughout their lives and never possess spots like the channel cat. The blue cat's tail forks deeply like the channel cat's, and its scientific name, *Ictalurus furcatus*, translates roughly as "forked tail fish-cat." The anal fin has 30 to 35 rays with a bottom margin that is straight and tapered like a barber's comb. The back profile, from the dorsal fin forward, is straight and steeply sloped, giving the blue catfish's head a distinctive, wedge-shaped appearance.

Blue cats utilize current more than any other catfish. They feed in swift-water "chutes" or in pools with distinct currents, using the moving water as an aid in foraging. Blues are more selective in their feeding habits than channel cats. Younger, smaller fish reportedly feed on even smaller fish, crayfish, leeches, fresh-

The channel cat (top) has the deeply forked tail characteristic of most catfish, and is usually olive-colored with round, dark spots. Anal fin rays range from 24 to 29. The blue catfish (second from top) has a distinctive, wedge-shaped back from the dorsal fin forward. Its anal-fin rays range from 30 to 36. Whites (second from bottom) are the smallest of the cats and have an anal fin ray count of 19 to 23. Flatheads (bottom) have a shovel nose and an almost square tail. Its extremely short anal fin counts 14 to 17 rays.

America's Big Cats

water mussels, small clams and aquatic insects. Adult fish feed primarily on other fish such as shad, herring, carp, drum, bluegill and even other catfish. Blues are particularly fond of crayfish.

Although blue-catfish populations have declined over the past century, some true giants still haunt river and reservoir depths. In December 1976, three commercial anglers, plying their trade on Tennessee's Fort Loudon Reservoir, hauled a 130-pound blue into their boat. In 1970, a 100-pound giant was taken in Kentucky, and a 100-pound, 8-ounce monster was snagged in Nebraska. In 1990, a 90-pound blue was pulled from the tailrace below Guntersville Dam in Alabama. The all-tackle, rod-and-reel, world-record blue, according to IGFA, is a 109-pound, 4-ounce behemoth taken from South Carolina's Cooper River by George A. Lijewski in March 1991.

The average blue catfish taken by today's angler probably weighs 3 to 15 pounds, although 40-pounders are not uncommon. Yet, the giant blue, an elusive quarry shrouded in mystery and mystique, inspires many of America's most diligent catfishermen.

The White Catfish

White cats are somewhat rare to most North American anglers because they inhabit the smallest, natural range of all catfish. Often called the "Potomac cat," whites, at one time, had been limited to the Atlantic coastal states—from the Chesapeake Bay region southward to Palm Beach, Florida—and a few of the gulf states westward to Texas. They have been successfully introduced into many of California's waters, as well as numerous "pay lakes" across the country.

Whites, the smallest of the cats (other than bullheads), usually weigh only 1 or 2 pounds. The world-record white catfish, a 17-pound, 7-ounce specimen caught in 1981, was taken from Success Lake in California by Chuck Idell.

In appearance, white catfish are very similar to channel cats, although they are never spotted and do not grow as large. Counting the rays on the anal fin will positively identify the white cat. It should have 19 to 23. Although whites often possess the olive or bluish coloration of the channel cat, they typically display a sharp demarcation between the darker color of the side and the creamy-white belly. Some whites also appear to be mottled with milky, pale gray to dark blue splotches.

Like the channel cat, white cats will tolerate swiftly flowing streams, but prefer more sluggish currents like that found in marshes and bayous. Whites also tolerate brackish water, and thus are often found in the lower reaches of coastal rivers where other cats are absent.

One great thing about white catfish is that they are gluttonous feeders. They will strike virtually any bait offered to them. That, and the fact that they are not as nocturnal as the other catfish, has made them quite popular in "pay-to-fish" ponds. Because white cats are so similar to the other North American cats, they will only be discussed when necessary. For the most part, whites are basically channel cats that often live in more brackish water. Catching them is no different than catching channels.

The Flathead Catfish

The flathead, an unusual looking cat, is rarely confused with any other member of the catfish family. Its head is quite wide and flattened, thus the name "flathead." The eyes, which are rather small and seemingly flat, accentuate the flathead's shovel-nosed appearance. It is the only catfish with a square, rather than forked, tail. And, its lower jaw protrudes beyond the upper jaw. The anal fin is short with 14 to 17 rays. The flathead's back and sides range from a pale, yellow color to light brown with darker brown or black mottling. However, this mottling often develops poorly in larger adults taken from waters with a high turbidity. The fish's belly coloration runs from pale yellow to a creamy white color. The squarish tail's upper lobe is typically lighter colored than the lower lobe. This is most evident in smaller individuals. Younger flatheads are generally darker colored with bold, distinct mottlings, while larger fish are often more subdued. Common names for the flathead include the mud cat, yellow cat, appaloosa cat, shovelhead cat and the Johnnie cat. Its scientific name, *Pylodictus olivaris*, means "olive-colored mud fish."

The flathead came from the large rivers and tributaries of the Mississippi, Missouri and Ohio River basins, from southern North Dakota south into northern Mexico. Because they do well in most impoundments and grow to enormous sizes, flatheads have been stocked outside their native range.

Flatheads seem to be more nocturnal than the other cats. In their native riverine habitat, flatheads will remain in a deep, quiet

This flathead taken by the late Otis (Toad) Smith, outdoor writer and catfishing expert, was estimated to weigh nearly 50 pounds.

26   Complete Angler's Library

pool during the day, then move into shallow water riffles at night to forage. Biologists say that large adults often have a favorite resting place where they can be found each day unless disturbed. Flatheads are vicious, solitary predators, demonstrating an overwhelming preference for live fish. The dead-, cut- and stinkbaits that often catch omnivorous channels and blues will rarely produce a flathead. Flatheads have been observed holding quietly on the bottom with their enormous mouths opened wide until a smaller, hapless fish investigates the curious cavity or simply wanders a bit too close. Flatheads hold around wooden snags. However, because these fish are solitary and territorial, any given snag is apt to produce one fish, or perhaps two. If the territorial invader is small enough, it will be eaten; larger fish will be chased out of the area.

Flatheads are North America's second-largest catfish, exceeded only by the blue cat. Five- to 10-pounders are commonly caught, and 30- to 40-pound fish will rarely warrant a mention in a hometown newspaper. The world record, a 98-pound flathead taken from Texas' Lake Lewisville Floodgate, was caught by William O. Stephens in June 1986. Although flatheads lack in appearance, they offer wonderful tablefare.

3

Catfish Through The Year

Like all of God's creatures, catfish must endure a wide variety of seasonal changes in their world. Through the years, anglers have learned, in general terms, how catfish cope with these environmental fluctuations.

In a sense, catfish are a slave to their surrounding temperature. Because they are poikilothermic, or cold-blooded, catfish have a body temperature that closely approximates the surrounding water. Their metabolic level, as well as their activity level, is closely tied to water temperature and, as a general rule, is directly proportional to it. In other words, catfish feed more often in warmer water than they do in a colder environment.

Through The Winter's Chill

Just as anglers often retire to the comfort of a cozy couch during the coldest weeks of the year, catfish also withdraw from the bitter cold. Catfish cannot escape their confinement to the frigid waters, but they can cope.

As a general rule, winter is a time of lethargy for the catfish, a period of relative inactivity that may actually approach something resembling hibernation. (Not a true hibernation, but a period of almost virtual inactivity and markedly decreased metabolic rates.) River-bound cats typically spend their winters in deep holes, often lying motionless behind rocks which break the river currents. Scuba divers swimming through the icy depths have observed catfish lined up in a row, head to tail, apparently reducing the

Pre-spawn runs of river-bound catfish can produce excellent results such as this nice cat taken by the author. They will be much harder to locate when they're holed up for the spawn.

Catfish Through The Year

current flow against each individual. Lake-bound cats retire to the sanctuary of deep water, though they normally do not have to contend with a swift current flow.

As the winter begins to break and flowers start to bloom, the catfish's activity level also begins to increase. At first, the cats simply begin moving about in their deep-water sanctuary. Shortly thereafter, they will start roaming, often trailing after the smell of a decomposing carcass of some creature that perished over the winter. This early spring season is perhaps the best time of year for using traditional "stinkbaits." Animals and fish that died during the winter begin to decompose rapidly as the water warms. Cats grow accustomed to tracking down these easy meals; they follow scent trails.

The Catfish Spawn

One of the most interesting segments of the catfish's life cycle is the spawning period. This phase spans at least two months and includes not only the act of laying eggs, but an upstream, and then (usually) a downstream, migration. For many anglers, this period provides some of the finest catfishing of the year. During this period, a few anglers enjoy the opportunity to actually wage war, hand-to-hand, with a catfish of monstrous proportions in a sport called noodling or graveling. But, many anglers, unfortunately, find this the most difficult time of the year for catching catfish—a difficulty that stems from a simple lack of knowledge regarding the catfish's life cycle rather than poor angling skills.

The catfish's spawning season can be divided into three relatively distinct phases: the pre-spawn, spawn and post-spawn. The pre-spawn period begins in the spring when water temperatures approach 60 degrees. The long winter has left the cats famished, and the rapidly warming water now spurs the fish into an active search for food. Typically, pre-spawn catfish swim upstream, a migration similar to the white bass' spring run and the sauger's winter migration. Unless impeded by falls, locks or dams, river-bound catfish may go a few miles upstream, although reports of migratory swims in excess of 100 miles have been documented. During this migration, catfish feed constantly, fueling their vast energy expenditures and storing energy reserves for the rigors of the approaching spawn.

Fishing is grand during this pre-spawn run. River holes seem-

Catfish aren't afraid to travel during their annual pre-spawn migratory runs. In many cases, the reason they don't travel farther during this run is because their route is blocked by a dam or waterfall.

ingly offer a limitless supply of catfish; catch a mess of cats from a good hole one day and chances are good that it will be restocked overnight. When a dam or other obstruction impedes their upstream journey, enormous schools of catfish—channels, blues and flatheads combined—congregate just below the impasse. Anglers often capitalize on this unique situation, and daily catches in excess of several hundred pounds are possible.

As water temperatures move into the mid-70s, the upstream migrations begin winding down and the cats begin searching for nesting sites. Many catfish anglers suddenly lose track of the fish. The catfish that seemed to be everywhere slowly begin disappearing. (Favorite holes may produce a few fish, but it is obvious that things have changed.)

Generally speaking, catfish spawn when water temperatures

climb into the 70-degree range. Biologists say that among genetically-close species, fish tend to spawn at different times, in different areas, or both. "These factors are called Reproductive Isolating Mechanisms (or RIMs)," says Ed Carroll, a district fisheries biologist in Kentucky. "The different species of catfish developed through these RIMs, and now continue to maintain their specific genetic integrity because of them."

The extended spawning periods of all catfish species generally overlap in most areas. And, cats all spawn in the same basic manner. Why, then, do catfish rarely hybridize, or cross-breed between species? The answer lies, perhaps, in the catfish's extraordinary sense of smell and unique communication ability. Pheromones are chemical signals that are produced in the mucus covering the catfish's skin, secreted by the gonads (ovaries and testes) and exuded by other organ systems, as well. Catfish can smell or taste pheromones that other catfish release. Researchers have discovered that catfish not only recognize individuals of other species through these pheromone indicators, but can remember the identity of a particular individual of their own species after a time lapse of three weeks!

Catfish also use sound to communicate. Most species can create a grating noise when moving their dorsal and pectoral spines. The fourth bone in the Weberian Apparatus (see Chapter 4) can vibrate against the gas bladder, creating a humming noise that functions as a reproductive isolating mechanism. This maintains genetic integrity during the spawn. Catfish make a particular sound that is species-unique. Individuals apparently utilize this signal to locate genetically-compatible partners during courtship and sexual-display behaviors prior to the actual spawn.

Another spawning factor is the size of mature catfish. Scott Hale, a Kentucky fisheries research biologist, says, "Channel cats often mature sexually at a length of just 8 to 10 inches, while blue cats rarely mature until they reach a length of about 22 to 25 inches, or a weight of 10 to 15 pounds or so."

Catfish spawn over a wide range of time and water temperature. This leads researchers to believe that factors such as the length of the day or night (referred to as the photoperiod) and an internal, biological clock or calendar are just as important (if not more) than water temperature.

For the most part, all catfish spawn in the same, basic manner.

Persistence is the key word in tracking the big cats (in this case, flatheads) during their spring, pre-spawn migratory runs. They are going to be tough to find at times, but the reward will be well worth the effort.

Catfish Through The Year

The males locate a suitable nesting site, preferably a cavity with a single opening. Hollow logs, empty cans and drums, undercut banks, natural cavities in rocky bluffs, old muskrat holes, crevices in chunk rock and riprap and even old appliances serve as adequate nesting sites. Seclusion and semi-darkness seem to be major factors in nest selection. Occasionally, catfish will spawn in a depression. It is not unusual to look over a bridge spanning a stream or shallow river and see cats nesting in discarded auto and truck tires. Some fish will migrate into small streams and feeder creeks, often venturing into water that barely covers their backs. Curiously, in the typical, bowl-shaped farm pond, lacking any sort of suitable nesting site, catfish will not normally spawn. The female simply reabsorbs the eggs. And, if they do spawn, predation of the eggs and newly hatched fry is so great that few baby cats will survive. (The addition of artificial spawning cavities will prompt the cats to spawn and help protect their progeny from predators.)

Once the male locates an appropriate site, he enters the cavity, enlarging it if necessary to accommodate both him and the female. Shortly thereafter, the female enters the nest and, after a brief courtship wherein the male swims over the top of the female and rubs her gently with his barbels and belly, lays a large, gelatinous mass of eggs. The male then fertilizes the egg mass with a spray of milt. The female soon abandons the nest (or may be driven out by the male), leaving the male to guard and care for the brood. In some instances, though not common, the female may assist in the rearing process.

The male catfish is a wonderful parent, caring for his charge diligently and without fail. For the first seven to 10 days, or until the eggs hatch, the male rests on top of the egg mass with his anal and pelvic fins vibrating rapidly to circulate water over the eggs and keep silt from settling on them. After the eggs hatch, the fry remain in the nest for another week or so under the male's constant protection.

In his role as guardian, the male catfish is vicious. Anything approaching the nest will be attacked, and perhaps eaten if small enough. This characteristic catfish trait has given rise to a form of catfish catching called noodling or graveling. The fearless "noodler" wades about in the shallows, probing every nook and cranny with his hands. A large catfish will typically inhale the noodler's hand, with which the noodler grabs the catfish's gill

This angler has successfully dragged a nesting catfish out of its den. The author discusses this unique (and highly controversial) technique, called noodling or graveling, in greater depth in Chapter 19. Some states do not allow this practice.

plate and prepares for an awesome game of tug-of-war!

Anglers who have grown fond of their hands and fingers can still take advantage of the catfish's protective instinct. By working a bait of some sort along a potential spawning area, like a riprapped bank, scores of cats may be pulled from their cave-like nests. Of course, these tactics present a moral dilemma for conservation-minded anglers who are dedicated to preserving the quality of our fisheries. Prudent fishermen who keep only what they need should not forego this spectacular opportunity, but should enjoy it while practicing catch-and-release with their excess fish.

After spending their first week of life under the protection of their father, the tiny catfish will leave the nest. Some studies say the father will continue to care for the brood for a few more days, but most biologists believe that the father and fry go their separate ways upon leaving the nest. Interestingly, first-year, fry survival is much greater in dingy water than in clear water, probably because the young are more exposed and more visible to predators in clearer waters.

As the spawn ends, the post-spawn period begins. Basically, this is a time when the cats, exhausted from the rigors of the spawn, begin moving toward their summer haunts. Often the fish will simply ease out into the current and drift downstream. Many cats who previously migrated into small creeks and feeder streams will make their way downstream to a larger river. Because this post-spawn period is a recuperative phase, the catfish rest often and expend only small amounts of energy.

Anglers need to remember that the catfish's actual spawn extends through a period of several weeks, perhaps as long as two months in some locales. Because the males spend roughly two weeks in the nest, and the females usually only a few days, it should become obvious that all catfish in any given area do not spawn at the same time. Thus, there are always feeding cats somewhere—all you have to do is find them!

The Stability Of Summer

As the recuperative, post-spawn period begins to wind down, the catfish will eventually make their way into deeper pools which offer cover, shelter from the current and quick access to shallower feeding grounds. The cats settle into predictable, behavior patterns, and anglers enjoy the stable fishing patterns that extend well into autumn.

Forage is plentiful through the summer months, although catfish often leave their deeper haunts during the night to roam the shallows where the majority of their food sources are located. Big flatheads spend their days in deeper holes typically associated with rough cover. At night, the "mud" cats ease into the shallows, often scouring the swift-water riffles in a river or stream, hunting the live fish they prefer. Blue cats prefer reposing in deeper river holes during the day, moving into the heads (or forward sections) of those holes at night, feeding in swift-water chutes that facilitate their forage gathering. Likewise, channel cats spend their days in deeper sanctuaries, although they tend to roam at night.

In the summer months, catfish actively feed sometime after

the sun has set. This is not to say, however, that cats cannot be caught during the day. Catfish, specifically big catfish, become rather opportunistic in their feeding habits. Present a bait to a big cat, even if he is not in a feeding mood, and he will probably pounce on it. Also, catfish feed more than just once a day. Although the major feeding periods may occur after dark, catfish feed actively (to some degree) during daylight hours.

Fall: The Wind-Down To Winter

Autumn months represent a declining activity level for catfish. In general terms, catfish will slowly gravitate toward the largest, deepest holes available, anticipating the coming cold. While the fish may move upstream or downstream, downstream movements are probably most common. These movements are rather casual affairs, and not the en masse migrations that occur in the spring. Feeding activity is still high, and will remain so until the water cools dramatically.

As autumn ends and the nights grow cold, catfish will begin grouping in large numbers in the deepest, available holes. Initially, they will make foraging runs into the shallows of surrounding areas. However, these feeding jaunts typically slow down and activity centers within the hole itself as winter blows into town.

4

Catfish Senses, General Anatomy

"Why, Grandmother, what big eyes you've got," said Little Red Riding Hood.

"All the better to see you with," said the wolf.

"Why, Grandmother, what big ears you've got," said Little Red Riding Hood.

"All the better to hear you with," said the wolf.

"Why, Grandmother, what a big nose you've got," said Little Red Riding Hood.

"All the better to smell you with," said the wolf.

"Why, Grandmother, what big teeth you've got," said Little Red Riding Hood.

"ALL THE BETTER TO EAT YOU WITH!" growled the wolf.

—From the fairy tale, Little Red Riding Hood.

Designed to survive, to thrive in an often hostile environment, the catfish is a marvel of sensory perception with a set of senses that are unequaled by any other freshwater fish. So acute are the perceptive abilities of this fish that it can feed, hunt and even flourish in total, absolute darkness. Many anglers and outdoor writers have labeled the catfish as primitive. But, as you shall soon see, primitive is no more of an accurate adjective for a catfish than short is for a giraffe.

The Sense Of Sight: Little Eyes, But ...
Catfish have evolved as fish of rivers, an environment that

Cutting bluegills into bait-sized pieces may not be the most fun in the world, but it will draw a response from catfish. These fish have an uncanny ability to detect blood and fluids oozing from the bait.

Catfish Senses, General Anatomy

typically yields waters of higher turbidity, or dingier waters, than lakes and ponds. The evolutionary process gifted the catfish with an extraordinary sense of smell; a sensory system that aids the catfish when feeding in muddy water far better than excellent vision ever could.

The catfish's eye is quite small when compared to its body size, and tiny when contrasted with the eyes of other fish that are exclusively predacious. From this, many anglers wrongly assume that catfish have poor eyesight, or that they do not utilize their sense of vision when feeding. The fact is, catfish frequently feed on live fish such as shad, carp, drum, bluegill and assorted minnows, and they often utilize their eyesight to capture this kind of agile prey. The catfish's vision is probably not as acute as that of the trout, bass, walleye or bluegill, but it is nonetheless a vital sensory organ system. In a clear-water environment, vision is probably the catfish's key sensory organ when foraging for live fish or other forage.

The eye of the catfish has evolved to complement their night-feeding habits. Catfish have a structure in the eye that functions much like a mirror, reflecting gathered light back over the sensory cells on the retina. It is this same structure that gives walleye their distinctive "marble-eye" appearance. Because the eye of the catfish is much smaller than that of the walleye, the reflective aspect of the catfish's eye often goes unnoticed by anglers. Ultimately, this reflector increases the catfish's vision in periods of low light intensity (at night or in muddy water).

Fisheries biologists have determined that "rods" and "cones" are present in the catfish's eye in roughly equal numbers. Rods provide a kind of black-and-white vision in low-light conditions, while cones offer chromatic, or color vision in daylight. Although there are no major studies of color vision in catfish, all indications show that it does exist. One catfish angler who puts stock in the catfish's ability to see colors is Bob Holmes, a dedicated outdoorsman from Trenton, Tennessee. For years, Holmes has placed half-inch sections of plastic worms on his hooks along with his baits, primarily to provide a splash of color.

"The piece of plastic worm makes the bait a bit more buoyant," Holmes says. "But, I believe it functions most effectively as an attractor to the catfish, something to get the fish's attention. We have done informal studies on the technique and, invariably,

Colored, plastic worms added to bait hooks can bring a quick response from hungry catfish. In many cases, the brighter the plastic, the better cats like it.

the angler using the piece of plastic gets a bite more often." Holmes' favorite color is red, although he also uses blue worms in clear water and chartreuse ones in muddy water.

Sound, Hearing And The Lateral Line

Like most fish species, the catfish's sense of hearing may be attributed to two different physiologic systems: the ear and the lateral line. The catfish's ear, much like our own, senses true sounds while the lateral line detects water displacements near the fish.

The catfish's ears are located on either side of the head, although there are no openings to pinpoint their location. With an ear enclosed within their flesh, how can catfish hear? That is an interesting question, and one that is best answered by the physics of wave propagation and density.

Considering that sound is waves traveling through water, and that a fish's flesh is (for the most part) water, the fish can be considered to be acoustically transparent. In other words, the sound waves travel through the fish's flesh as if it were not even there. Therefore, fish do not need external openings to their inner ears.

The catfish's inner ear consists of three semi-circular canals (giving the fish a sense of balance and body location) and three pouch- or sac-like structures that serve as the organs of sound reception. These sacs, which are lined with cells covered by hairlike projections, contain dense nodules of calcium carbonate called otoliths. The hairlike projections are in contact with the otoliths, or ear bones.

When a sound wave passes through the catfish, it causes most of the tissues to vibrate in a uniform manner (because most tissues have a uniform density approximating that of water). The otoliths, however, are much more dense than the surrounding tissue, providing resistance to movement. Thus, they vibrate at a different rate than the surrounding tissue whenever a sound wave passes through the fish. The otoliths' movement causes movement of the hairlike cells lining the ear, stimulating a series of nerve endings which send a message—or a "sound"—to the brain.

By itself, the catfish's inner ear is rather inefficient because of the relatively small difference in density between the otoliths and the surrounding tissue. Catfish, however, belong to a large group of fish that possess a unique system called the Weberian Apparatus that serves to better their sense of hearing. In an extraordinary evolutionary marvel, the first four bones of the spinal column have been modified over millions of years to create a kind of chain (the Weberian Apparatus). The first bone touches the inner ear on either side of the head, while the fourth bone touches the fish's swim bladder. When a sound wave passes through the fish and strikes the gas-filled swim bladder, it actually resonates within the bladder and transfers to the inner ear through the chain of vertebral bones.

Intimately tied to the catfish's sense of hearing is the lateral line, a sensory system that detects minute water displacements around the fish. The lateral line is a series of tiny canals with lots of nerve endings that run along the sides of the fish at roughly the mid-line. Similar canals exist around the eye, down the lower jaw and over the head. A series of hairlike projections within the lateral line canals bend in response to water displacements, thus stimulating nerve endings that transmit a message to the brain.

The lateral line detects low-frequency sounds or vibrations, that cannot be detected by the fish's ear. The catfish's lateral line receives those sounds or vibrations, and messages sent to the brain correlate and give meaning to the fish. Creatures swimming through the water, scuttling across the bottom, plopping onto the surface or stomping along the riverbank, all create low-frequency vibrations in the water that the catfish's lateral line detects. The catfish uses this system to detect, identify and localize prey, potential enemies and members of its own kind (primarily for schooling and sexual display behaviors).

In the catfish's watery environment, the lateral line might best be considered "a sense of touch at a distance." Although it is an advanced sensory organ, the lateral line helps the catfish the most in locating prey within one body length from itself; rarely does detection go beyond five body lengths.

Bob Fincher, a catfish guide from Nixon, Texas, ranks catfish as one of the most alert fish in freshwater. "The catfish has a super sense of hearing," he says, "and you can bet your bottom dollar that he will most often know that you are there. Cats really aren't all that spooky, I guess; I mean they won't run if you make a sound. But, I do believe that if you make a lot of unnecessary noise, you are apt to upset the fish and then they certainly won't bite as readily."

Some catfish have another means of detecting both prey and predators. Unfortunately, this method is not yet fully understood by research biologists. Tiny pits concentrated on the head but also scattered along the body apparently are able to detect extraordinarily minute changes in electrical currents. Most creatures radiate electrical impulses. Apparently, catfish can detect living organisms by simply swimming close to them and monitoring the electrical changes with their pit organs. This can be done in turbid water, in total darkness or even when the prey is buried in sand or mud! Although this ability has been discovered in many catfish species around the world, it is not known to what degree large, North American catfish utilize this amazing sensory system.

The Senses Of Smell And Taste

In humans, the senses of smell and taste are closely related.

Our nose picks up odor molecules floating in the air, while our taste buds receive signals from molecules suspended in liquids or saliva. These two senses are even more closely linked in the catfish because molecules that can be smelled or tasted suspend in water.

The catfish probably has the most advanced smell-detection system of any fish that swims in freshwater. Unfortunately, it's a complicated system and not yet fully understood by leading researchers. Basically, water going through the nostrils passes over a series of olfactory receptor cells. Olfactory folds line the inside of the nasal passage. These folds increase the tissue's surface area and the number of olfactory receptor cells coming into contact with the water.

Dissection of various species has revealed that catfish have more olfactory folds than other freshwater species. Because of this, the catfish is believed to have the most advanced "smeller" in the freshwater arena. Channel catfish, for example, have approximately 140 folds, while largemouths, smallmouths, rainbow trout, crappie and bluegill may have only 12 to 24 olfactory folds. As fish of a certain species grow in size, the number of olfactory folds increases. Thus, the sense of smell apparently grows more acute as the fish ages.

Catfish, like sharks, seem particularly competent in detecting very minute traces of amino acids in the water. Amino acids are protein building blocks in living organisms. They are released into the water (in bodily fluids) whenever an organism is injured. Blood is particularly rich in amino acids, and the catfish's ability to detect, follow and locate blood and its source is legendary.

One interesting adaptation of the sense of smell in fish is the alarm substance. In the late 1930s, an Austrian biologist, Karl von Frisch, discovered that an injured minnow dropped into a tank housing a school of the same species somehow alerted the other minnows, which then became agitated and rapidly retreated. Later, he demonstrated that a chemical—the alarm substance—is released whenever the skin of a fish is lacerated. That chemical, which alerts other specie members to potential danger, is detected through the sense of smell. The cells producing this alarm substance have been named "club cells," and biologists have learned that catfish have larger club cells than most other fish. This leads us to believe that this communication is highly advanced in the catfish. Apparently, some predatory fish, like the

Complete Angler's Library

Nares, or nostrils located between the uppermost barbels and the catfish's upper jaw allow water to pass over the fish's olfactory folds, accounting in part for the cats' acute sense of smell.

catfish, can detect this alarm substance secreted from members of other species, and then use that information (a scent "trail") to focus on a potential meal.

While the catfish's sense of smell is useful at a distance, the sense of taste becomes more important when the catfish moves in close to a potential food source. Fish possess bundles of receptor cells known as taste buds, which are stimulated from substances— tastes—dissolved in the water. Most fish have taste buds dispersed primarily around the lips, mouth and throat. But, catfish also have many taste buds located in the eight barbels, or "whiskers," around the mouth. Cats even have some taste buds in the skin all over the body. While most fish must actually put a bait in their mouths to taste it, catfish need only brush it with their barbels or their body.

Catfish have eight barbels, two on the upper jaw, four on the lower jaw and one on each side of the upper jaw. These barbels, or whiskers, are sensory organs that help cats smell and taste.

The catfish's extraordinarily developed senses of smell and taste are no secret, and catfish anglers have capitalized on it for centuries. Smelly baits producing so-called scent trails have long been popular. To this day, fishermen still cut, pound, mince and slice their cut baits, increasing the flow of bodily juices that seep into the water, in order to attract a feeding cat. Astute anglers have learned the value of "chumming" or baiting their favorite holes, enticing catfish into the area. (See Chapter 12.)

Over the past decade, the sportfishing industry has adopted angling scents that are poured or sprayed onto lures and baits. These potions attract fish, or convince a potential "biter" that this offering is indeed something to be eaten. Although the actual value of these potions is still a topic of debate, some catfish experts literally swear by them. Given the all-encompassing catfish nose, they might very well be extremely beneficial. If the ingredients are indeed attractive to catfish, the addition of these liquids to an otherwise dry bait, such as a typical dough bait, might help the catfish locate the morsel more easily.

Researchers have made some interesting discoveries about the intelligence of fish. Dr. Loren Hill, director of the Oklahoma

Complete Angler's Library

University Biological Research Center, says, "Catfish are one of the most easily trained fish that we have ever studied. Their learning ability approaches that of the largemouth bass, and may actually exceed it. In fact, we can train catfish to respond to the sound of a bell in less than a week. I would have to say that the intelligence of the catfish is extremely high in relation to other freshwater fishes." Other studies have confirmed Dr. Hill's findings.

A primitive fish? Hardly. No way. Not even close. Catfish are masters of their environment and more in tune with their world than virtually any other fish that NAFC Members will encounter in North American waters.

5

The Catfish's Environment

Catfish evolved through the millennia as a native of North America's natural rivers and streams. As we have already seen, the catfish's unique senses ideally suited it for life in the often turbid waters of a river. Catfish adapt more easily than most other freshwater species. As a consequence, they have found their way into the giant impoundments of the United States, as well as into the tiniest farm ponds scattered across the country. Their natural ranges have been greatly expanded through stocking projects, and now virtually every state in this great nation is home to at least one catfish species. And, wherever they happen to find themselves, catfish usually thrive—a reflection on their great ability to adapt.

The Aquatic Environment

Oxygen, a life-sustaining gas, is essential to both animals and fish. While animals living on land obtain oxygen from the atmosphere, fish get their oxygen from the water. Even though water is 88 percent oxygen (by weight), that oxygen is bonded to hydrogen and can't be used by fish. Fish utilize free oxygen molecules released from the photosynthesis of aquatic algae and vegetation and dissolved into the water; a smaller portion of the dissolved oxygen in water comes from its surface contact with air.

This exchange of gasses—gathering oxygen from the water and expelling carbon dioxide—is a function of the gills which serve as a fish's respiratory organs. Basically, water is drawn into

Construction of electrical power plants along rivers over the years has resulted in ecological changes which have affected catfish. Warm water discharges create noticeable imbalances.

The Catfish's Environment

the mouth where it then passes through the gills and exits through the gill cover, or operculum. A fine network of blood vessels housed in the gill membranes transfers carbon dioxide from the blood to the water while oxygen is extracted from the water and absorbed into the bloodstream.

The oxygen requirements of fish are determined, first of all, from genetic makeup. Different species have different oxygen requirements. In addition to genetics, oxygen requirements also are determined from water temperature. As water temperature increases, so does the fish's metabolism, requiring more oxygen to meet the fish's increased demands.

The catfish's survival ability during periods of low-oxygen concentration is well documented. This has led many anglers to wrongly assume that catfish simply do not need a healthy, well-oxygenated environment. To thrive and flourish, cats need a dissolved oxygen level equivalent to that of bass or walleye. If dissolved oxygen levels in an area fall below optimum levels, catfish will, however, survive much longer than most other fish.

Specific internal modifications have evolved in catfish that simply help them survive and endure environmental changes that may kill other, less developed species.

The swim bladder (also called an air or gas bladder) serves primarily as a hydrostatic organ. In effect, the swim bladder makes the fish somewhat neutrally buoyant so it does not have to swim constantly to maintain a specific depth. The fish regulates the gas amount in the bladder, according to its depth.

Most species regulate the gas amount in the bladder in one of two ways: Fish, like trout and salmon, regulate their swim bladder when gulping air at the surface and directing it into the bladder, or expelling air from the bladder in something akin to a burp. Other fish, like bass and crappie, regulate the gas volume in the bladder through a complex series of blood vessels that either dump gas into or withdraw gas from the bladder.

Catfish, however, can regulate the gas volume in their swim bladder in both manners. This ultimately results in a complex mechanism that enables cats to survive when most other fish would succumb to oxygen deprivation. "In time of need, catfish can actually obtain oxygen from the air in their swim bladder," says Ed Carroll, a fisheries biologist for Kentucky Department of Fish and Wildlife Resources. "When the levels of dissolved oxy-

Dispensing chemicals into rivers stresses fish which depend upon extracting oxygen from the water. Catfish can, however, extract oxygen from the air, also.

gen in the water are too low, catfish can rise to the surface and gulp air into the swim bladder. Oxygen from the swim bladder is then absorbed through the fine network of blood vessels surrounding that organ."

Occasionally, you may see fish such as bass or bluegill gulping or "piping" at the surface. Although it looks like they are gulping air, they are actually trying to lay their gills in the thin, oxygen-rich interface between the air and the water.

"Many times, when you take a catfish out of the water," says Caroll, "you can find him still alive hours later. The reason for this is two-fold. Catfish can actually extract oxygen from the air in their swim bladder. Additionally, the catfish's gill structures are more rigid than most other species. When you pull a bass or a walleye or virtually any other gamefish, for that matter, out of the water, its gill filaments will collapse so that air cannot pass through them. But, as long as the catfish's gill membranes remain moist, it can withdraw oxygen from the air."

Needless to say, this is a grave, last-ditch effort that is not at all conducive to the catfish's well being.

In addition, catfish can absorb oxygen through their skin, according to Dr. Loren Hill, a professor of zoology and director of the Oklahoma University Biological Research Center in Norman. "Through a complex process called cutaneous respiration, catfish can extract oxygen directly through their skin, even in the absence of water," Hill says. "Catfish are survivors. They are not primitive creatures by any means; they simply developed several physiological mechanisms that allow them to survive long after other fish have died, and this often leads people to believe that catfish are just primitive creatures."

The temperature of the catfish's environment varies widely throughout the year; yet, catfish seem to cope extraordinarily well. Occasionally, Northern anglers catch cats through the ice, even though catfish lie almost dormant in deep-water pools during the coldest weeks of the year. The summertime surface temperatures in some of the finest Southern fisheries often reach well into the 90s, although catfishing remains productive.

If catfish could adjust a thermostat in their environment, studies have suggested, they would select a water temperature somewhere between 75 and 85 degrees. That is perhaps the ideal temperature for feeding, growth and activity for North American catfish. Nevertheless, channel cats do especially well in cooler waters. In the Northern range, for example, the water temperature seldom reaches the 80-degree mark; yet, some of the finest channel cat fishing is found there. As temperatures grow inordinately warm (into the upper 90s or lower 100s), the fish become stressed, grow lethargic and seldom eat. The same is true when water temperatures fall to near freezing, except that these fish are probably not physically stressed.

There has been some speculation that genetic sub-types may exist in the catfish family just as they do in the black bass family. The Florida strain of largemouths, for example, can tolerate warm water better than their northern-strain cousins. Perhaps this explains why channel cats in Canada grow in waters that rarely reach their laboratory-determined, optimum temperature.

Catfish pH Preference

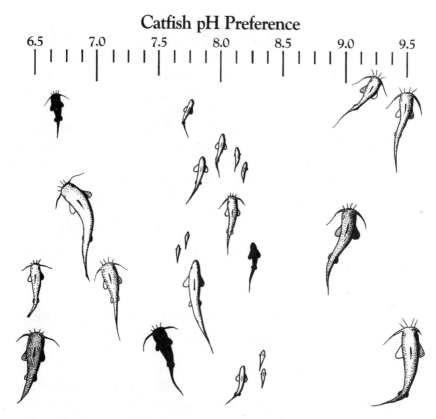

Catfish are adaptable to the widest range of water pH. Most gamefish have a limited range. The catfish's extraordinary adaptability belies its primitive image.

Although catfish can tolerate various water conditions, they (except for the white catfish) apparently dislike brackish water. Catfish are freshwater fish. It seems they cannot, or will not, tolerate a high saline (salt) content in their environment. In many of the Eastern coastal rivers and streams, populations of blues, flatheads, and/or channel cats will dwindle at the point where the water turns brackish. White cats, however, may be found well into the salty waters. In the Southern coastal marshes and bayous where white catfish are absent, other cats may occasionally be found in brackish waters but are most often small and stunted.

Catfish seem to be more tolerant of variations in the water's acidity or alkalinity (measured as the pH) than many other species. Actually, pH is a scientific measure of the hydrogen-ion concentration in the water, a critical component in maintaining the proper chemical balance in a fish's body. The ideal pH level for most predatory gamefish is 7.5 to 8.5, although catfish thrive in a range from 7.0 to 9.0. As a general rule, bottom-dwelling fish can withstand a poor pH better than other species.

"In our studies, we have observed catfish surviving at a pH of 2.7," says Dr. Loren Hill, "which is extremely low, or acidic, for any living creature. The reason that catfish can withstand a lower pH than most other fish is because they have the ability to extract oxygen in ways other than through their gills." (The efficiency of a fish's gill system relates to the water's pH.) However, catfish will vacate waters with a poor pH for more favorable conditions. "We have learned that catfish utilize avoidance behavior when moving about in their environment," Hill says. "They will avoid unfavorable conditions and continue searching for more agreeable surroundings."

The Greatest Threat

While catfish rank among the most adaptable of creatures, there are those environmental changes to which the catfish cannot adjust.

What is the greatest threat to North American catfish and their environment? Of the millions of different species that have lived and died on this planet, no single animal has changed the environment as much as man. The environment and its silent constituents have paid the price for some of that change.

A trillion pounds of hazardous waste were produced in this country alone in 1990, some of which will find its way into our aquatic ecosystems. This includes dioxin, considered by many to be the most hazardous substance. Herbicides and pesticides drain from farm fields in water runoff, making their way into tributaries. Scores of hazardous chemicals and heavy metals including mercury filter into our waters from waste sites, illegal dumps and industry discharge pipes. Polychlorinated Biphenyls, or PCBs, which were used as plasticizers, flame retardants and dielectric agents until their ban in 1979, still haunt us, contaminating many of our lakes and rivers. A favorite catfishing site, the tailrace below Fort Loudon Dam in Tennessee, bears signs warning anglers of the contaminate, and of the dangers of eating catfish from those waters. Nevertheless, catfish anglers haul boatloads of fish from that section of the Tennessee River virtually every day.

Pollution takes its toll on all fish. Even though catfish can adapt to undesirable environments better than other fish, there are some places that catfish can't survive in, either.

The Catfish's Environment   55

A clean, healthy environment will produce nice catfish like this one which Tom Mann caught in a small pond.

Then, there is acid rain. Nitrogen oxide emissions from automobile exhaust and sulfur dioxide emission from coal-burning plants account for the vast majority of acid rain and snow in the United States.

Aquatic ecosystem contamination is not limited to chemical pollutants. Soil erosion results in siltation, carried by water runoff into creeks and rivers, then into lakes and reservoirs. As this dirt (or silt) settles to the bottom, it fills the lake, causing it to grow more shallow as it ages. Silt not only clouds the water, but it decreases sunlight penetration through the water, as well. Ultimately, this inhibits the growth of beneficial algae and plankton, or the bottom of the food chain for all aquatic species. Additionally, excessive siltation impedes the reproduction of fish by covering productive spawning areas and settling on unhatched eggs (eggs that will never hatch).

Organic wastes are released into our waterways primarily through the sewage treatment plants of large cities, but also enter watersheds as slaughter-house effluents and nitrogen-rich, agricultural fertilizers carried by runoff. For a time, anglers often reap the benefits of a fertile fishery. Ultimately, however, the numbers of shad and bluegill, catfish and bass, may dwindle or perhaps disappear altogether.

The catfish is uniquely gifted to withstand the rigors of a harsh environment, and to a certain degree, catfish can better contend with the cruelties of polluted waters than most other gamefish. Some chemicals enact their evils by killing the catfish outright. Others are more insidious. Some poisons actually invade the catfish's genetic makeup, causing misshapen progeny and failed spawns. Others may cause tumors, especially on the catfish's lips.

Because catfish, for the most part, dwell on the bottom of lakes and streams, they are especially at risk to those chemicals that are heavier than water. Heavy metals and PCBs are a problem in many regions of the country. These pollutants contaminate and infect not only the catfish, but all creatures that eat catfish. Luckily for us, most of these contaminates are bound into the fatty portions of the catfish and most may be removed through careful fish-cleaning practices.

Catfishing
Equipment

6

Rods, Reels And
All That Gear

Darrel Van Vactor sits in his boat over a creek channel in Kentucky Lake. The tip of his long, wispy-thin spinning rod dances a jig, evidence that his baitfish is being eyed by a hungry predator. Suddenly, the rod jerks downward until its tip touches the surface of this sprawling lake. The 12-pound line screams from the spinning reel, but Van Vactor calmly turns the boat with the trolling motor and begins following the fish. He fights the giant with a lover's gentle touch, tenderly urging the fish upward through the depths without testing the limits of his delicately thin monofilament. Some 30 minutes later, a 68-pound blue cat is netted at boatside.

While Van Vactor is fighting his fish in Kentucky, Ken Nelms drifts over a channel break in South Carolina's Santee-Cooper reservoir system. Armed with a stout, beefy rod, a reel that might serve admirably as a stump-pulling winch, and 30-pound monofilament, Nelms bounces a large chunk of cut herring down the break, leading into a deep-water pool. Without warning, the rod nearly escapes his grasp as if it snagged a Volkswagen running downhill under a full head of steam. Nelms sets the hook and, immediately, the monstrous fish turns toward a fallen tree whose branches protrude from the water like the bony fingers of some watery giant. Instantly Nelms reacts, raising the rodtip high overhead and leaning away from the fish, using his own weight to help stop this runaway cat. Stretched tight as a banjo string, the thick monofilament sends a spray of water droplets through the air. But,

Catfishermen who are targeting the big cats usually will opt for heavy-duty tackle so they're not caught short. A long, stout rod and heavyweight spinning reel are a popular combination.

it holds, and Nelms turns the fish away from the ominous wooden sanctuary. About 10 minutes later, a 63-pound blue is hoisted into the boat.

These two catfish guides use tackle that might be considered near the opposite ends of the tackle spectrum. While Van Vactor opts for light tackle in the open-water expanses of Kentucky Lake, Nelms selects heavy-duty gear for Santee-Cooper's treacherous, cover-rich channel flats. Both anglers accomplish the same task, success based not only on their angling competence but also on proper tackle selection for their respective jobs.

Historically, catfish anglers have used whatever tackle they might have on hand. In most parts of the country, that meant bass fishing gear. And, while bass tackle is perfectly acceptable for various catfishing chores, experts have discovered that fine-tuning their gear to match a specific catfishing task will usually put more fish in the boat.

Catfishing Rods

Selecting a proper rod-and-reel combination should be based on the fishing style, or technique that will be performed. Run-of-the-mill bass gear will suffice for tossing a gob of nightcrawlers into your favorite stream. Switch to a big live bait, however, and you need a fairly good-sized outfit just to handle your terminal tackle rig. Likewise, if you routinely fish for, and catch catfish less than 10 pounds or so, your bass tackle will meet most of your needs. But, if you decide you would like to land a leviathan (and eventually you will), arm yourself appropriately.

A Case For Longer Rods

Long fishing rods, those measuring at least 7½ feet—or the customary size of the bass angler's flipping stick—seem to be a better choice for most catfishing tasks than a shorter rod. Here's why:

• A long rod allows you to move more line more quickly, and with the same effort, than does a short rod. Ultimately, this results in surer hooksets and increased line control.

• Casting distance increases with a longer rod. This is an advantage when shore fishing.

• Long rods allow you to "lob" a bait a respectable distance. With a short rod, you might have to resort to a wrist-snapping, cracking-the-whip type of cast to achieve the same distance, an

A good supply of weights and sinkers is a must if you're going to effectively fish for cats on the bottom or drift offerings through holes as this angler is doing.

act that will throw a soft bait off your hook.

• When using light line, a properly selected rod will bend parabolically in response to the catfish's fight. This puts more stress on the rod than on the line. This results in fewer break-offs and more fish boated. As a general rule, anglers hunting big fish with light lines need a very long rod properly mated to the "test" of the line. Ten- and 12-foot rods are often needed for this task, although you may have to resort to one of the European rods now on the domestic market.

• Long rods give you more "reach," or the ability to move your line in and around cover. Long rods will also help you keep an ill-tempered cat out of your prop.

• When drifting a bait underneath a float, a long rod lets you keep more of your line out of the water. This not only provides a

Rods, Reels And All That Gear   63 more accurate drift and a more natural presentation when stream fishing, but it gives you more control over your bait and a quicker response time when the strike occurs.

• Long rods, specifically those with a longer butt (lower handle section) provide the angler with more leverage. When battling trophy catfish, you will need all the leverage you can get!

Rod Composition

Today's fishing rods are made from various materials. Fiberglass, graphite or combinations of the two are the most popular.

Fiberglass rods have a "soft" action, compared to graphite rods. In other words, they bend more easily with the same amount of pull. Although fiberglass is more durable, it lacks the sensitivity of graphite. Few catfish anglers use fiberglass rods; however, some heavy-duty, saltwater "pier" rods constructed on fiberglass blanks are used by monster hunters.

Graphite rods tend to be "stiffer" and lighter in weight than comparable fiberglass models. They are also much more expensive. Graphite's major advantage is its remarkable sensitivity. A good graphite rod will conduct every quiver of an excited baitfish being eyed by something big and ugly, thereby letting you know something is about to happen! In essence, whenever sensitivity is important, whenever you are detecting bites through your sense of touch or feel, a graphite rod is a good choice. Graphite rods are not as durable as fiberglass or composite rods. Even though they rarely break when actually fighting a fish, their somewhat brittle nature makes them susceptible to quick, sharp bends or blows to the rodtip.

Rods constructed of a fiberglass/graphite composite may be the best all-around choice for catfishing, especially those models with a relatively high percentage of graphite fibers. The graphite offers both strength and sensitivity, while the fiberglass provides a slightly softer action than 100-percent-graphite versions. These rods seem unbreakable, yet retain enough sensitivity to satisfy most anglers. They are especially useful when drifting or bottomfishing with the poles secured in rod holders and the reel's "clicker" engaged.

Baitcasting, Spinning Or Spincast Reels?

Because catfishing is traditionally a big-fish, heavy-line tech-

Most anglers consider a stout baitcasting reel a must for fishing big cats. It should have large line capacity, a line-out alarm or clicker, and it should be well made.

nique, baitcasting gear is typically chosen. For most catfishing situations, a baitcaster is the hands-down winner.

There are certain situations, however, when spinning gear should be used. Primarily, any time you use light line (anything less than 12- or 14-pound test) spinning outfits are preferred, since they handle smaller-diameter lines better. If you simply want to have a good time catching fish and would not be heartbroken if a bruiser snapped your line, traditional bass fishing spinning gear is fine. If, however, you are actually trying to land a decent-sized catfish on light line, you need to opt for a well-balanced, long-rod/spinning-reel outfit matched precisely to your line size. And, even then, you will have your work cut out for you! Additionally, spinning reels do not offer the raw power that baitcasting reels provide.

For the average American angler, spincast outfits rank highest in popularity. All are easy to use and remarkably simple to cast. Bob Fincher, a full-time catfish guide and blood-bait manufacturer from Nixon, Texas, uses large spincast outfits for all his catfishing. "Virtually anyone can cast these reels and feel comfortable using them," Fincher says. "If you select a good model—a big one with a decent line capacity and a good drag system—it will serve quite well as a catfishing tool. And, when you are using a soft bait, like congealed blood, spincast reels will let you make a relatively long, lob-type cast without throwing your bait off the hook." Spinning reels offer the same feature, however, spincast reels handle line in the 14- to 20-pound class much better than spinning outfits.

Ultimately, the choice is yours.

Better Baitcast Reels

When all is said and done, most dedicated catfish anglers will wind up using baitcasting gear for the majority of their angling assignments. In addition to quality, rugged construction, catfish reels should offer a "clicker" (also called a "line out" alarm) and plenty of line capacity.

A clicker is certainly one of the most important and useful features on a reel drafted for catfishing. It is used primarily when still fishing, although anglers who drift fish or slow-troll baits often consider it vital, as well. When used with the free-spool button, the clicker "clicks" audibly when line is pulled from the reel, thus informing you of a strike. Additionally, the clicker keeps a soft, steady tension on the spool, thereby preventing a fish from backlashing the reel when it runs with a bait. To use the clicker, simply push the free-spool button and engage the clicker switch.

To hold an ample amount of heavy line, catfishing reels should be of the wide-spool variety. Ideally, the reel should hold approximately 200 yards of 20-pound-test monofilament. Even if you opt for using 30- or 40-pound line, a reel of this size stores a sufficient quantity for most catfishing tasks.

A Note On Fishing Lines

Fishing line is often called the "weak link" between angler and fish. When you are dealing with fish that routinely break the 30-, 40- and even 50-pound marks, it is extremely important that you

Catfishermen have lots of choices in line selection. Most experts agree that cats aren't line-shy, so you might as well go for the thick stuff. Use 25- to 30-pound-test as a minimum for big cats.

use line of the highest caliber. Today's premium monofilament lines offer a superb blend of tensile strength, limpness, abrasion resistance and knot strength. Stick with name brands that you know and trust.

For all-around catfishing use, 17- to 20-pound-test monofilament is an excellent choice. If, however, you hunt the big boys, 25- or 30-pound line should be a minimum. The overwhelming majority of catfish experts reports that cats are not "line shy," so you might as well arm yourself appropriately. After all, you do not hunt elephants with a .22 caliber rifle.

Remember that catfish have hundreds of sandpaper-like teeth that can saw through a thin line in seconds. For this reason, many experts use a heavy, 30- to 50-pound-test leader attached to their smaller, main line whenever they are catfishing.

Rods, Reels And All That Gear

The fishing area plays a crucial role in line selection. If you comb a river filled with craggy rocks and heavy wooden cover, obviously you will need a strong line that resists abrasion. But, in the open expanse of a reservoir's offshore flat, you can land a whale on 8-pound test—if you've got all day to spare!

In strong-current areas, like the tailraces below giant, hydro-electric dams, spool your reel with one of the new ultra-thin monofilaments. These whisper-thin lines, because of their markedly decreased diameters, cut the current much better than normal lines of the same test; yet, they are just as strong.

Also, line visibility should be considered when purchasing line. If you enjoy night-fishing by the purple glow of a black light, you will certainly want to choose a fluorescent line. Some of the super fluorescent, bright green and yellow lines are used and recommended by experts. Three-time national catfish champion Ken Nelms uses a super-bright, green monofilament that stands out like Darth Vader's light saber, even in the blazing sun. "I typically use six rods all of the time," says Nelms, "and this bright line helps me keep track of everything at a glance." If you like the advantages that a bright line offers, yet worry about the catfish being spooked, simply add a short, clear monofilament leader to the end of your line.

Terminal Tackle

Like the bass angler who totes a tackle box stuffed full of crankbaits so he will have a specific plug on hand when he needs it, the catfish angler must carry his own tackle box, albeit a smaller one! The catfisherman's box is a simple affair, consisting of various hooks, sinkers and swivels and sundry odds and ends.

Catfish hooks are chosen in response to two variables: the size of the catfish you are likely to catch and the size of your bait. Necessarily, anglers need a wide assortment of hooks. On occasion, you might find a use for hooks in the No. 4 to No. 1 size range, but for most catfishing tasks you will probably use 1/0 to 4/0 hooks. Confident monster hunters using giant baits to attract giant catfish will find many uses for hooks in the 5/0 to 7/0 range.

Generally speaking, your standard-style, run-of-the-mill fishing hook (provided it is top-quality) works for most situations. For larger catfish, consider stocking a few Kahle-style hooks. The wide bend or "gap" of this hook design provides plenty of room for a large live or cut bait. For trotline use, opt for a long-shanked hook that facilitates quick-and-easy hook removal.

Some catfish experts think hooks with an offset bend (ones that automatically turn when a fish bites) dramatically increase hooking success. Long-shanked versions of these hooks are available and are good for trotlining. Because catfish biting a trotline bait must hook themselves, this automatic rotation increases hookups to some degree.

Generally speaking, forged steel hooks are probably the catfish angler's best hook choice. While stainless steel hooks provide added corrosion resistance, attracting the trotline angler, they are often softer or more brittle than their carbon-steel counterparts. Catfish have thick, tough mouths that can be difficult to penetrate. Always carry a file, a whet rock or some type of tool for sharpening hooks and make a habit of using it. There are various premium hooks now available that are wickedly sharp. Several Japanese firms market such hooks, and at least one American company offers chemically sharpened hooks. Although more expensive than ordinary fishing hooks, these models can be of real value to the catfisherman.

Catfish anglers will find various uses for treble hooks and should keep a few models and sizes in their tackle boxes at all times. These hooks work well with congealed-blood and chicken-livers baits. Trebles in sizes No. 4, 6 and 8 are most suited to catfishing tasks. Several companies offer treble hooks with a coiled wire fitted around the hook's shank, and they have no equal for use with soft-dough baits. When the dough or paste-bait mashes into the coiled wire and packs into a ball around the shank, it is held more firmly, helping the angler keep these soft, squishy baits on the hook.

Because catfish are, for the most part, bottom-dwellers, you will need an assorted supply of sinkers. Sinker weight depends on bait buoyancy, water depth and current. As a rule, well-versed catfish anglers use only enough weight to keep their bait in place. For most catfishing chores, you will want various slip sinkers in weights ranging from ¼ to 1 ounce, some heavier sinkers (2 to as much as 6 ounces), for use in swift-water areas like tailraces, and a few split shots.

Slip sinkers are rigged so they slide freely on the line. They are typically kept away from the baited hook by a "stop," such as a swivel tied in place 18 inches or so ahead of the hook. Egg sinkers are probably the most snagless of all catfishing weights and a good choice in still water. However, they tend to roll around too much in river current. In current, opt for bell sinkers (also known as dipsy, bankcasting, or bass-casting sinkers), pyramid sinkers or walking sinkers like those commonly used by walleye anglers. Split shots are used most often when drifting baits in streams, typically beneath a bobber.

You will also want a few swivels in your box. Catfish roll a lot when hooked, so many anglers habitually add a swivel to their rigs. Swivels, often utilized as a "stop" between a slip sinker and the hook, do not crimp or damage your line, and they always stay in place. One word of caution: Avoid those cheap, brass-plated, tin snap swivels at all costs. A big cat will tear one apart in a heartbeat. Snap swivels, of any kind, have very little use in this game. When fishing for big cats, purchase top-quality, ball-bearing swivels. Three-way swivels are utilized in some catfishing rigs, so stock a few of those, as well.

In addition to all of this catfishing gear, most experts keep a stock of bluegill-catching supplies stashed somewhere in their boats to assist in bait collection.

A Word Of Advice

Ultimately, the most important consideration when purchasing catfishing tackle is quality. Pound for pound, catfish "pull" as hard as anything that swims in freshwater. As catfish expert Bob Fincher says, "You just never know what is going to bite when you go catfishing. It is not uncommon to catch 2-pounder after 2-pounder, then suddenly find that you've hooked up with a 50-pound giant. The only insurance you can get when catfishing is to buy quality tackle, and I can't stress that enough. Every piece of tackle that you use, especially your rods, line and terminal tackle components should be of the finest quality available. After all, you just never know what is going to bite!"

Remember, it wasn't raining when Noah built the ark.

Catfishing Rigs

Because catfishing, for the most part, requires a bottom-oriented fishing style, you will want to learn about various terminal tackle rigs that will match the varying conditions you are

Slip Rigs For Catfish

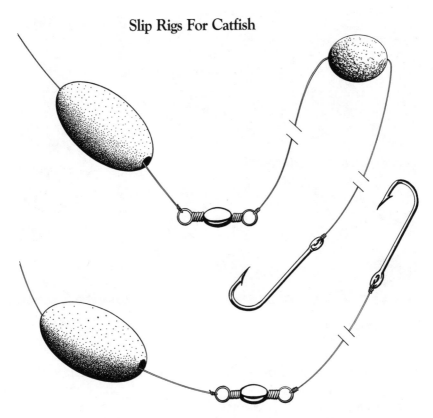

Two versions of slip rigs that are often used for cats are shown in this drawing. The top version incorporates a small, balsa float that lifts the bait off the bottom.

likely to encounter. (Floats and their accompanying rigs are discussed in Chapter 13.)

Set Rigs

Simply stated, set rigs are cast into the water where they sink to the bottom and stay until a catfish finds the bait. With most set rigs, the hook is located in front of the sinker—or attached to the line in front of the sinker—to retain sensitivity.

The basic set rig is a catfishing standard. A double surgeon's loop knot ties into the main line, and a snelled hook ties to the resulting loop. When fishing for smaller cats, many anglers add a couple of extra baited hooks.

The three-way set rig is a better choice for hunting big cats than the basic set rig. A three-way swivel ties to the terminal end

This young angler, who happens to be the author's son, is learning early about slip rigs and various baits for serious catfishing. He's also prepared with a cutting board built into the bucket.

of your main line. A short section of light monofilament with a bell or pyramid sinker of the appropriate weight attaches to the lower ring of the swivel. Should the sinker become snagged or wedged between rocks, this light line breaks, releasing the rest of the rig. A length of heavy leader with a hook on the end attaches to the swivel's upper ring. This rig, when used with a heavy sinker, works well for vertical bottom-bouncing directly under the boat in a river or in the swift-water chutes of a tailrace.

Slip Rigs

Slip rigs are utilized by the majority of catfishermen in America. In essence, the slip rig allows the cat to take the baited hook unencumbered by the sinker's weight. Some anglers believe cats are less likely to drop a bait with the free movement that this rig provides. Others tout slip rigs because they improve the angler's ability to sense a bite.

The basic slip rig (with an egg sinker) works best in a still-water environment. The rig can be modified for use in current by simply replacing the egg sinker with a bell or pyramid sinker, although the next rig might be a better choice. Even though a split shot could be used instead of the swivel, most anglers opt for the swivel's security. Additionally, tying a swivel into the line allows the angler to use a heavy leader (attachment between hook and swivel) as insurance against line abrasion when fighting a hefty cat. Some anglers also add a glass or plastic bead between the sinker and the swivel, preventing the heavy sinker from banging against, and damaging the knot connecting the swivel to the main line.

The heavy current/heavy cover slip rig works better in those situations than the basic slip rig. In heavy current, the bell or pyramid sinker will not roll like an egg sinker. In heavy cover, the light line connecting the sinker to the main line will break if the sinker becomes snagged, releasing the rest of the rig.

Ken Nelms' version of the slip rig resulted from years of on-the-water research. Nelms allows his boat to drift with the wind, dragging this rig over productive structure such as stump fields, humps and flats bordering a channel. Nelms believes that big catfish prefer to feed upward, and the small float incorporated into his rig presents the bait at eye-level for the catfish. "That little crappie float may look unusual," Nelms says, "but my percentage of hooked fish has risen dramatically since I began using it. Also, the float keeps the hook above most snags, so I spend more time fishing and less time on hooks. I always use a leader made from 50-pound-test monofilament because a big cat's teeth and fins are murder on a line." Although Nelms prefers to drift or "slow troll" the rig, it is quite effective when still-fished on the bottom.

=====7=====

Sonar: Our Underwater Eyes

Catfishing, to many anglers, means finding a cozy little spot on a riverbank, building a nice campfire and tossing a gob of nightcrawlers or a chunk of chicken liver into the ambling currents. Chances are good that a nice fish or two will be caught. Nevertheless, it will be an enjoyable evening, because this is our catfishing heritage, the way our fathers and grandfathers spent time with us years ago.

Serious catfish anglers (the men and women who have vaulted the ancient craft of catching cats to something of an art form) know they must leave the lake shores and the riverbanks and hunt offshore structure if they want to be truly proficient in their endeavors. Like the quail hunter who relies on a brace of fine pointers, the catfish angler has his own bird dog: sonar.

No matter how deep or dark the waters, a good depthfinder can show us what is beneath the boat. We can see fish-holding structure, as well as fish.

Ultimately, sonar units become the most vital piece of equipment for dedicated hunters of these whiskered denizens of the deep. Without a depthfinder, catfishing becomes a game of chance. And, on our massive lakes and often enormous rivers, anglers failing to use a sonar unit to the best advantage literally stack the odds against themselves from the outset.

The Principles Of Sonar: How Does It Work?
Sonar units are, in simplest terms, sound-emitting devices

The first step in catching big catfish is finding them. The electronic gadgetry available today makes it a lot easier. A number of catfishermen use both flashers and liquid crystal units.

Sonar: Our Underwater Eyes

that measure distances through water. First developed by the U.S. Navy in World War II, the units were designed primarily to locate, track and determine the distance to an enemy submarine. The word *sonar* is a military acronym for SOund NAvigation Ranging.

Once installed in your boat and connected properly, a depthfinder operates on electrical power from your boat battery. When the unit is functioning, a minute electrical charge flows from the depthfinder unit through a coaxial cable into the transducer, which is usually mounted somewhere on the bottom of the boat. The transducer converts the electrical impulse into sound waves, which are then directed down through the water. A mark on the screen signifies the zero-foot mark, or the surface. The sound waves travel through the water and are reflected back to the transducer by anything dense enough to reflect them, be it a catfish or a minnow, a log or the bottom. These reflected sound waves are called echoes, signals or returns.

Reflected sound waves are received by the transducer and converted back into electrical impulses. Based on the time those impulses took to flow down through the water and return, run back up the transducer cable and into the depthfinder unit, images are processed and displayed on the screen at different depths. Because the speed of sound in water is known and remains constant wherever you go, the time span between the sound wave's origination and its received echo can be measured and correlated as a distance, or as a depth mark on your unit's screen.

Because the lake or river bottom is the most dense object sound waves will encounter, that echo displays as the widest and most distinct return on the unit. Soft, muddy bottoms absorb a great deal of the sound waves, thus causing the return to be rather narrow. Hard, rocky bottoms, on the other hand, reflect most of the sound waves, being displayed as a very wide return.

The sonar unit actually sends and receives one sound wave before the next is sent. Because water is a non-compressible medium, sound waves travel much faster and more efficiently through water than they do through air. In fact, sound travels at a rate of 4,717 feet per second through water, or just over four times faster than it does in air. Therefore, sonar units operate incredibly fast with most units sending and receiving approximately 10 signals per second. This assures you of complete coverage of everything under the boat (when operated properly). The sound waves spread out from the transducer in what is best described as a cone shape. As the depth increases, so does the bottom of that cone; thus, as water depth increases, so does the width of the area being scanned by the sonar unit. This has some very important ramifications that will be discussed later.

Sonar Displays

One common misconception among anglers is that one type of sonar unit is inherently more accurate than another. To some degree that is true, but not for the reasons people believe. All depthfinders—flashers, liquid crystal units, video sounders, paper graphs and digital displays—function in exactly the same manner. The *difference* lies in the way the information is displayed.

Basically, there are three types of sonar displays: the flasher, the picture-type display (which includes liquid crystal units, paper graphs and video sounders) and the digital display.

Flashers

The flasher is simply a box in which a light bulb spins rapidly behind a circular screen engraved with depth marks. When the unit senses a reflected signal, or return, the bulb flashes--or blips—as it passes the corresponding depth numeral.

Flashers were the first sonar units designed for angling use. And, for the past decade or so (or since the introduction of the liquid crystal display), doomsayers have been predicting the demise of these depthfinders. Because flashers are still relied upon by anglers as versatile units, and are available at an attractive price, flashers will be around for years to come, though the number of manufacturers offering them is dropping.

Most often, anglers use flashers to navigate a lake or river while running at high speeds. Because the data from a flasher is not "processed" by an internal microchip, its reports appear much sooner than information gleaned from any other depthfinder. Flashers are superb units for scouting: searching for structure, locating areas of deep, or shallow water and hunting for fish.

The flasher excels at scrutinizing the lake's bottom composition, determining whether it is hard or soft. Because catfish prefer a hard-bottom type, mainly rock, gravel or sand, this is an important step in locating probable fish-holding structure, or catfish themselves. Setting the flasher's sensitivity (or power, and some-times referred to as "gain") properly helps anglers accurately judge the bottom composition by studying the width of the bottom's re-turn. A hard bottom, because it reflects most of the sound waves, appears as a wide return. A mud bottom, because it absorbs many of the sound waves, is a more narrow return.

A flasher's bottom signal, or return, is quite wide. This can be confusing when determining true bottom depth. As a rule, the true bottom is located at the uppermost, or shallowest end, of the lake bottom's return signal. For example, say you are sitting over a rocky bottom that gives a constant bottom blip at 32 to 38 feet. The true bottom depth is 32 feet, not 38.

Flashers are also quite capable of locating fish. Individual baitfish will be indicated by a thin blip, whereas larger fish show up as a wider blip. As a general rule, a top quality flasher offers a resolution—the ability to separate targets—of about 6 inches. Thus, two fish less than 6 inches apart will generally show up as one large blip. Especially important for catfish anglers, this also is true when fish are holding directly on the bottom. Typically, flashers will not separate a catfish from the bottom return when

Flasher units are available with different depth scales. So, if most of your fishing is done in shallower water, the unit on the left probably will work best for your type of water.

Covered Catfish Images

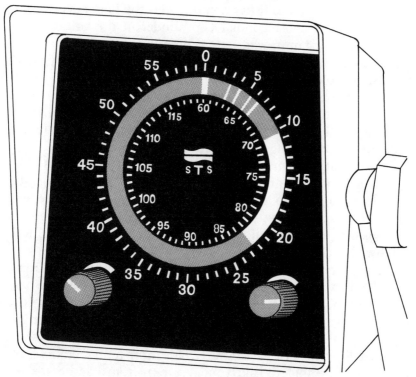

Fish signals on a flasher can, at times, be obscured within a wide response band from structure. In this example, it is impossible to find fish that might be holding in 12 to 22 feet of water.

the fish lies directly on the bottom, unless the bottom is extremely hard, flat strata—and the unit is perfectly adjusted. However, this combination is very rare.

Also, the flasher does not indicate fish holding along a steep drop-off. When the flasher's transducer is positioned over a drop-off, the shallow and deep ends of the drop, as well as all the bottom signals in-between, will appear on the screen as a single, wide blip. Any fish holding along that drop would be lost in the overlapping signals. This also happens when you're searching for catfish along a bottom littered with big rocks—catfish holding beside a rock will be lost in the return. Although picture-type displays will show fish holding along a depth break, obviously no sonar unit of any kind can possibly show a fish holding underneath a boulder or a rocky ledge.

Liquid Crystal Displays

First introduced to fishermen in 1984, the liquid crystal unit has become the most popular depthfinder in the country. Although those first units were extraordinarily crude by today's standards, angler acceptance was overwhelming then and continues to be strong today.

For ease of use, the liquid crystal unit has no equal. By simply pressing the "on" button, the unit's automatic functions will paint a picture of the aquatic environment under the boat, including accurate depth readings and illustrations of suspended fish. These units are relatively small in size; most are of reasonable cost. Because they do not require paper, they are inexpensive to operate; they draw very little power from your battery; and unlike flashers, the unit's display shows you where you have been. These are all features that endear the liquid crystal unit to a number of American fishermen.

Liquid crystal units, called LCRs or LCGs by manufacturers, actually draw a picture of the area under the boat. When the boat is in motion, the right-hand or trailing edge of the display (the new information being presented) shows you what is under the boat, while the picture on the left portion of the screen shows you the area you have just passed over. This short-term memory is often vital to the angler. Take your eyes away from a flasher for just a second and you may miss the drop-off you were searching for. The LCR, on the other hand, keeps this information on the screen for several moments. This feature is particularly helpful to an angler following a contour line or trying to maintain a specific depth. It also tells you where you have been—all without having to keep your eyes glued to the screen.

The picture displayed on the liquid crystal unit is a conglomeration of small dots, or pixels, that are activated whenever an echo is returned to the transducer. The number of vertical pixels on the screen governs the display quality: the more vertical pixels, the better the display will be. Small numbers of pixels result in a boxy-looking display, while a large number provides a more realistic appearance. A unit's resolution directly relates to the number of pixels available. The unit's cost is more often directly proportional to the number of pixels available on the screen than to the number of features offered.

The heart of the liquid crystal unit is a small computer chip, or

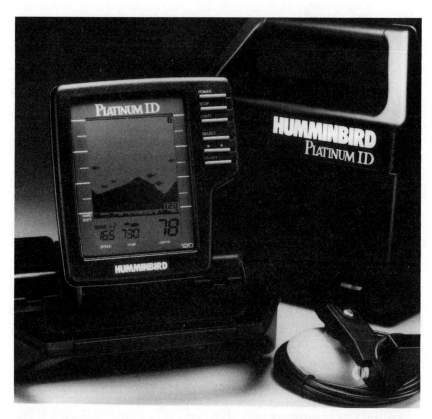

Liquid crystal display units such as this one provide a lot of information in easily digested form. The information at the right of the display is the most current. This unit has the advantage of being portable.

microprocessor, which correlates the data received from the transducer and displays it on the screen. The use of a computer chip makes a whole array of features available on LCRs. All are simply programmed into the chip and can be called upon, usually through a menu of sorts, by the angler. Some of the more useful features include zoom capabilities, a "bottom lock" which zooms in on the bottom of the lake to simplify fish identification, fish alarms, depth alarms, temperature gauges and even the capability to merge with a Loran-C navigational unit.

Today's finest LCRs offer a grayline feature (similar to paper graphs) that helps the catfish angler locate bottom-hugging fish. Although most liquid crystal units now offer a lighted or back-lighted display, catfish anglers who ply their craft after dark should be certain that a unit offers this feature; otherwise, the depthfinder is virtually useless after sundown.

The Paper Graph

The paper graph unit offers the most detailed display of any of the depthfinders. Capable of separating targets as close to each other as one inch apart, the best paper graphs offer a resolution that is approximately five times better than the finest liquid crystal units. For serious fishfinding, the paper graph has no equal.

The paper graph's display is created by a heated stylus that moves up and down over a special thermal paper. While the paper is fed from right to left, the stylus races up and down along the display's right-hand edge. Whenever the unit receives an echo, the stylus inscribes a corresponding mark on the paper. The paper graph is state-of-the-art angling equipment, and can describe everything under your boat in near-infinite detail.

Because the display is etched onto paper, these units also offer a permanent record of the aquatic environment. The unit can be stopped at any time, so notes can be scribbled on the paper. The paper can be saved in a notebook, offering a valuable reference chart for future use.

One of the most useful features of the paper graph, especially to the catfish angler, is the grayline. When set properly, the grayline feature separates all other objects from the bottom return, and from each other. Thus, catfish lying directly on the lake floor can be readily identified, and fish holding close to each other can be defined as separate fish. The grayline is the finest interpretation feature available on depthfinders today, and operates best with the paper-graph detail.

Paper graphs are not perfect. Because they require special paper, running the unit extensively can become rather costly. Changing paper can be a chore in rough water or foul weather, and takes time away from your fishing. The stylus, an inexpensive item often included with rolls of paper, will wear out and must be replaced periodically. The unit must be cleaned occasionally because it will become grimy from carbon residue created when the thermal paper is inscribed by the heated stylus. Some anglers might find the intricate control panel on some of the paper graphs to be intimidating. But, in reality, most are rather easy to use after you've become familiar with the unit. The units also are among the most expensive traditional depthfinders. In the end, however,

Complete Angler's Library

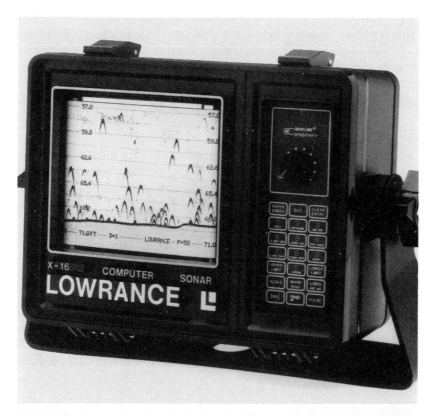

Paper graph units provide the best detail of any depthfinder unit, and the information can be retained for later use. A drawback is that replacement paper is costly, and it runs out at the worst possible time.

most dedicated catfish fanatics will opt for a paper graph.

Video Sounders

Using a cathode ray tube much like the picture tube in a television set, video depthfinders offer the most colorful displays in the industry. Also, these units offer superb resolution and a number of features.

Video sounders, however, haven't been well received by freshwater anglers. Although color units are quite expensive, monochrome versions are available at prices comparable to the better liquid crystal sounders. But, the units are rather large and cumbersome, requiring considerable space for installation. Many are not waterproof, and most are difficult to read in bright sunlight. (However, an inexpensive sun-shade or visor that clips onto the unit can virtually eliminate that problem.) Anglers also look upon the video unit—specifically its picture tube—as being quite fragile. In reality, however, most manufacturers mount the tube in a free-standing, shock-absorbing bracket that insulates it from the jolts and jostles of rough-water runs.

Digital Displays

Digital depthfinders, literally, are nothing more than that. They simply give you a readout of the depth underneath your boat. They are basically an aid to navigation. Flashers offer more information, are easy to use and cost a lot less.

Transducers And Cone Angles

If you compare a depthfinder to a short-wave radio, the depthfinder's transducer functions like the radio's transmitter and antenna. The transducer contains a small crystal, converting electrical energy into sound waves which move through the water in ever-widening circles, or cone-shaped patterns. The sound waves, returned, or echoed, back to the transducer are converted into electrical energy and transmitted to the depthfinder for processing and display.

The sound wave produced by the depthfinder transducer actually looks more like a water balloon suspended from one end, but the cone shape is more easily visualized and discussed. Different transducers emit sound waves at different cone angles which govern the amount of area covered underwater. The cone angle is actually the angle between the outside edges of the sound cone.

For all-around freshwater use, a transducer operating at approximately 200 kilohertz with a 20-degree cone angle is almost ideal for defining structure and locating fish. At 200 kilohertz, you have a selection of transducers with different cone angles. Wide cone angles (say 30 to 45 degrees) will not penetrate as well into greater depths, nor will they show drop-offs as accurately as a more narrow cone angle. Narrow cone angles in the 8-degree range are available, but are used primarily with digital sounders, displaying no more than the depth. Transducers with narrow cone angles show only a very small amount of the area under the boat. This can create problems. At a depth of 100 feet, for example, a 20-degree cone provides information within a 35-foot diameter circle on the bottom, while the 8-degree-angle cone will only show in-

Varied Cone Coverage

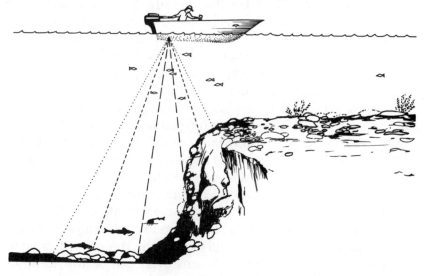

Wider angle cones cover a bigger portion of the bottom. It's important that the angler knows how much of the bottom he is actually seeing when passing over structure.

formation within a 14-foot circle.

Many anglers assume that their units show a wide area beneath their boat when, in fact, the amount of coverage is actually quite small unless a wide-angle transducer is used. With a 20-degree cone angle, a depthfinder's bottom coverage equals about one-third of the water depth. At 30 feet, then, your depthfinder would cover a circular area on the bottom roughly 10 feet in diameter. Knowing this helps the fisherman pinpoint fish, and present the bait quite accurately. Remember, the transducer represents the center-most point of bottom coverage.

With a properly installed transducer, a properly set depthfinder will show you both fish and structure under your boat. If you are adept with basic hand tools and follow the instructions, installing the transducer and depthfinder is not a problem. However, for a modest fee, most marine dealers will install the depthfinder for you. Once the depthfinder is properly installed, it is time to study your instruction manual and learn to use the unit. Mastering sonar takes time, concentration, research, practice, diligence and patience. Once the information is stored in your head, your fishing will probably improve dramatically.

Depthfinder Or Fishfinder?

Though generically labeled as depthfinders, most sonar units are accurate and impressive fishfinders, as well. Fishermen who have trouble locating fish on their sonar units probably do not know how to use their units properly. Any depthfinder will easily tell you the water depth. Unfortunately, many anglers use their depthfinders for nothing more than that.

While depthfinders may be able to pinpoint the location of a fish under the boat, they cannot tell you what kind of fish is down there. A knowledge of fish species, their habits and preferred locations will, however, give you some major hints when identifying those masked bandits under the boat.

To transform your meager depthfinder into a super fishfinder, learn to use the sensitivity setting. The sensitivity knob (or incremental buttons on some units) functions much like a volume control on a radio. Just as you would turn up the volume on a radio to hear a whisper, a depthfinder's sensitivity can be turned up to show the smaller, less dense objects underneath your boat. Increasing the sensitivity to the point where all objects in the water become visible on the depthfinder's screen often results in a cluttered display. Although some may find this clutter annoying, it is the best way to accurately "see" into the dark depths beneath you.

Sensitivity should be adjusted to match the changing depths and bottom conditions. When the boat is above a weedy or muddy bottom, the sensitivity needs to be increased to compensate for the sound waves absorbed by the soft bottom structure. In deeper water, also, the sensitivity should be increased because those sound waves have to penetrate the depths and return.

Often, when the sensitivity is set correctly, a second bottom echo will appear at roughly twice the depth of the true bottom. No cause for alarm. This is because the sound waves created by the transducer reflect off the bottom, return to the surface, reflect off the surface, hit the bottom once more, and finally, strike the transducer on the second bounce. Occasionally, there may be three, four or even more bottom echoes.

Depthfinders have noise-reduction filters, usually called the suppression controls, which reduce unwanted signals. Typically, this suppression reduces the signals from surface clutter, cavitation interference and electrical interference. Showing up on screen may be signals from microscopic plant and animal organ-

These two anglers are fine-tuning their depthfinder's sensitivity setting so that they can get a clearer, less-cluttered view of what's beneath the boat. Most new units have automatic sensitivity control which can be overridden if desired.

Sonar: Our Underwater Eyes   87

If the depthfinder unit is properly adjusted, the images on the unit's screen should look a lot like this. Newer units are designed for hands-free operation, but occasionally adjustments will be necessary.

isms, air bubbles that may be trapped around the transducer (which may be improperly installed) and "static" from the boat's electrical system.

A depthfinder's suppression controls can help eliminate the cluttered display associated with these problems by changing the pulse length, or the frequency, of the sound wave transmitted by the transducer. The problem with suppression controls, however, is that suppression reduces your depthfinder's ability to discriminate between objects that are close together. With suppression increased, two fish might merge into a single return. A baitfish school might become a monstrous fish beneath your boat.

Learning to operate the suppression controls correctly is a matter of trial and error. As a general rule, do not increase the suppression unless it's absolutely necessary. When running your boat at high speeds, you often have to bump up the suppression controls to obtain a clear bottom signal. But, when you slow down and resume fishing, be sure to decrease the suppression. Usually, if you need to use the suppression controls routinely, particularly when fishing, you probably have a problem with your electrical system or an improperly installed sonar unit.

Sonar signals at the cone's edge must travel farther to reach the transducer than those located at the same depth in the cone's center. The classic "arch" or "hook" display of fish on a depth-finder is the result of this phenomenon. (Note, however, that these arched fish signatures happen only when there is some movement by either the fish or the boat or both.)

It would be nice if sonar units showed exactly where a catfish is; however, that is just not possible. Nevertheless, these tools perform remarkably sophisticated tasks and point anglers in the right direction. Better than that, they show, within a few feet, the approximate location of fish. From there, it is all up to you.

8

Catfishing Tools
Of The Trade

Armed with just a few poles, a box of hooks and a couple of sinkers, anyone can wander down to the creekbank, dig a few worms or catch some bluegills, and then catch cats. However, serious, dedicated anglers require a little more gear. No self-respecting catfisherman, for example, would dare leave the dock without a depthfinder. As you grow with the sport, you will find a need for more specialized gear and, like sliced bread and indoor toilets, you will wonder how you ever lived without them.

A Better Bait Bucket

Whether you fish from the bank or from a boat, you will need something for storing your bait, as well as something to cut it on. In addition, bank anglers need something for carrying their gear while descending to the riverbank.

One superb solution is a simple bait bucket made from an old, plastic, 5-gallon bucket. These can be found at most building sites (drywall mud and industrial paints come in these buckets), and sometimes at fast-food restaurants that buy mayonnaise in large quantities.

To make the bucket usable, simply cut a half-moon-shaped piece of wood to fit across half of the bucket's opening. Hardwood is best, although pine will work. Don't use plywood. The wood should fit snugly into the bucket's throat. Now, a few holes are drilled through the bucket's side and into the wood. Insert screws

A bait tank with an aerator is an essential investment if you're fishing for cats with shad as live bait. The tank should be round so that the shad won't crowd into the corners and die.

Catfishing Tools Of The Trade   91

to hold the cutting board in place. Next, drill a pilot hole or two and use a jigsaw to cut knife-holding slits wherever desired.

If you want a lid for the bucket, put the cutting board an inch or two below the bucket's top edge. However, setting the cutting board flush with the top of the bucket is a better choice. The completed bucket can be used in several ways. Some anglers net shad and dump them into the bucket for use later as cut bait. This not only keeps your bait, cutting board and fillet knife all in one convenient location, but is neat and clean, as well. Also, you can store all your scents and dough baits in it, or use it to carry your gear to the creekbank. Every year or so, or when needed, simply remove the worn-out cutting board, replacing it with a new one.

Slick as shooting fish in a barrel!

Lighting Up The Night

Most catfishing activity occurs after the sun sets so you will need battery- or fuel-powered lights.

Every catfish angler must have a lantern. Tradition demands it. For illuminating a wide area of the creekbank and giving you that cozy, camping feeling, nothing beats a good gas-powered lantern. Place the lanterns well behind you and your rods so you are not inadvertently and temporarily blinded by the light. Also, when you're fishing from a wooded shore, your rods can be put in holders near the water, the lantern in front of a nearby tree, and you can sit well behind the tree. The rods will be illuminated, but the light won't shine in your eyes. If you like more light on your boat and don't mind the bugs, a good lantern holder that clamps on the gunwale or attaches to a rod-holder mount does the job. If the bugs are bad, the light can be suspended out over the water with a tubular extension.

When night fishing from a boat, a powerful spotlight is a must. Most connect into your boat's 12-volt system via a lighter socket, although a few are actually rechargeable. They come in candlepower (C.P.) ratings, ranging from 200,000 all the way up to 1,000,000 (that is one bright light!). Portable spotlights are not only valuable in operating the boat, running trotlines and checking limblines, but necessities when you're searching a pond, lake or river for catfishing jugs.

Although they are considered accessories for the nocturnal bass angler, black lights help the late-night catfisherman, as well.

A powerful (and reliable) spotlight is better than a flashlight when you're trying to keep track of your line while fishing after dark.

These 12-volt gems emit a soft, purple glow that will light up a monofilament line with fluorescent pigment. Ten-pound test glows like an anchor rope, and 30-pound test looks like a mooring line for an aircraft carrier!

Black lights make line watching easier. The slightest line movement is easily seen; nibbles and bumps are glaringly obvious, and strikes are almost breathtaking. These lights help the angler stay on top of his fishing, letting him know, at a glance, what is happening on each of his rods. These lights also help you keep track of your lines. Any night-fishing veteran can tell you that keeping track in the dark of six or eight lines while drifting, slow-trolling or even fishing from an anchored boat is exhausting.

One black light will illuminate one side of an average-sized boat fairly well. Most anglers will need at least two, and some will use four black lights, two on each side of the boat. Be forewarned, though, that black lights are addictive. Once you try one, night fishing will never be the same again; it will be much better. Do yourself a favor and get a black light.

Whether you fish from bank or boat, you also will need a few flashlights for tying and baiting hooks, removing the caught cats, rummaging in your tackle box and hunting for that slimy shad that you dropped in the bottom of the boat.

Shad Stuff

If you do much catfishing in waters inhabited by shad or herring, you will probably need gear to collect and keep these wonderful baitfish. Like Bert and Ernie, shad and catfish go hand in hand.

First, you will need a cast net for collecting bait. These circular nets are one of angling's oldest tools; yet, they are as effective today as they were 500 years ago. In fact, nothing takes their place or performs the same job as elegantly. Yes, *elegantly*. Watching an accomplished net thrower is exciting. A gentle toss with a twist of the upper body sends the net swirling through the air until it opens, as gracefully as a butterfly, into a perfect circle.

Graceful net throwing is not accomplished overnight. These nets can intimidate some anglers. However, a novice can learn to throw one reasonably well in just one afternoon; but, throwing one perfectly will take a lot of practice.

Using a cast net successfully starts with selecting the right net. Even though differences between a poorly made net and a well-constructed one are not readily visible at first glance, the difference in performance between the two is quickly apparent. Quality nets cast easier, open flatter, sink quicker and last longer than cheaper versions.

Don Betts, an expert cast net engineer and North Carolina tackle-company owner, says, "Some of the things to look for when purchasing a cast net include a double selvage (a double stitching) of the lead line to the bottom of the net because much of the stress and strain placed on the net occurs at this point.

"Look for a sufficient number of sections in the net; cheap versions with just a few sections tend to parachute when you throw them, and that keeps the net from opening correctly and prevents it from sinking rapidly. Also, you will need at least one pound of

A cast net, if thrown properly, will make the taking of live bait a lot easier when you're fishing for cats. It takes practice, however, to be able to throw a net effectively like this.

lead for every foot of net. In the end, buy quality and you will not be sorry," Betts says.

Cast nets are sized in feet. Although not always correct, net size usually corresponds roughly to the net's radius. For example, a 5-foot net will have an approximate radius of 5 feet and, when thrown, will open into a circle approximately 10 feet across. (This holds true with quality-made domestic nets, but some imports, however, are typically sized larger than they actually are.) NAFC Members will find, as net size increases, it becomes more difficult to throw. But, it will also catch more shad with each throw. However, your chances of catching sufficient bait improves greatly because of the larger area covered with the bigger nets. The average, weekend catfish angler probably will find a 5- or 6-foot net sufficient for his needs. A guide, commercial fisherman or dedicated

A successfully thrown net should produce a haul of shad as this angler did with his throw. The author details the steps you need to follow in order to be able to throw a net properly.

enthusiast would probably use a 7- or 8-foot, or even larger net.

Cast nets come in various mesh sizes and a couple of different materials. For netting shad, a ⅜-inch mesh is nearly ideal. A net with a smaller mesh sinks too slowly, while a larger mesh allows small shad to escape. Or, the shad's gill covers will snag in the larger mesh, greatly impeding your bait-gathering efficiency.

"Nylon nets are almost a thing of the past," says Betts. "They are not as durable as monofilament nets, and they tend to become waterlogged and heavy. Monofilament nets, on the other hand, are very tough and will last for many, many years with reasonable care. Also, they cut through the water better than nylon, so they sink more quickly."

Most catfish anglers would be quite satisfied with a quality-made, ⅜-inch mesh, monofilament cast net in either a 5-, 6- or 7-foot size.

Betts recommends a simple way of throwing a cast net. "After attaching the handline loop around your right wrist," he says, "coil the handline in small coils and hold it in your right hand. Pull the draw strings (which pass through the middle of the net) upward with your right hand, making sure that they are not twisted or tangled.

"Now, grab the center of the net (usually a brass eyelet) and

Complete Angler's Library

slide it upward to meet the top of the draw strings. With your right hand, grip the net about a third of the way down from the top. Using your left hand, pick up the lead line (with weights on it) at one point and transfer it to the fingertips of your right hand (but do not let go of the net's mid portion).

"Now, using your left hand, grab the lead line at a point about 3 feet from where it is held in the other hand; you should end up holding the lead line in both hands. Then, simply swing the net from right to left using a twist of your upper body and throw the net with the right hand." (These instructions are for a right-handed individual; left-handed anglers need to reverse the entire process.)

If done correctly, the net should open into a flat circle before hitting the water's surface. Betts recommends practicing the technique in your yard using an old tire as a target. First, practice throwing the net so that it opens correctly. (It *will* take some practice.) Then, concentrate on hitting targets at various distances with it. To catch shad, you will need to be able to throw the net accurately over a range of moderate distances.

Shad are easily collected with a cast net in the swift water below most dams, but it is a hazardous task. In the tailrace's strong, turbulent currents, boats can move unpredictably. One unexpected lurch of the boat or a snagged net can put an unlucky angler in the raging water. Rather than tying the handline to your wrist as anglers usually do, slip it over a cleat on the boat. Pay attention and be extremely careful. And above all, wear a personal flotation device.

Sometimes, in tailraces, the shad are so thick that you can use a specialized dip net to collect your bait. These nets have a long handle, usually 7 or 8 feet or longer, and a platter-sized hoop holding a soft, small-mesh net. Look for shad holed up in the crevices between large rocks in swift water.

Where available, herring can be taken with a light spinning outfit and tiny white, yellow, chartreuse or green flies or grubs. Tie a $1/16$-ounce leadhead/grub or fly combination onto the terminal end of your line, then tie one or two $1/32$-ounce lures at 8- to 12-inch intervals above the terminal lure. Then, cast the rig into the tailrace currents, retrieving the rig slowly within a few feet of the surface. These baitfish strike with a vengeance and fight with a passion.

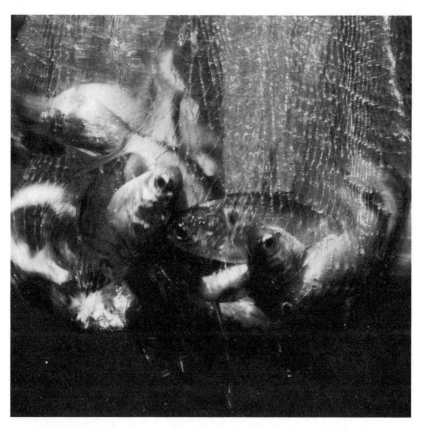

These shad will serve well as live bait, and sometimes even better as cut bait if they die in the bait tank. Their foul smell is especially attractive to lurking catfish.

Once the baitfish are collected, they must be stored. If you plan to use them as cut bait over the course of just one evening or so, you can simply toss them into the bait bucket described earlier along with some ice to keep them fresh and moist. If, however, you want to keep them alive for longer periods, you will need a shad tank. The shad is an extraordinarily fragile fish that can only extract oxygen from the water when moving. In a square livewell, shad will swim into the corners and die. (They're not only fragile, they're apparently stupid, as well!) For this reason, shad tanks are circular or oval-shaped, with no corners. Most hold 20 to 30 gallons of water. A strong agitator which is powered by the boat's 12-volt system and fits on top of the tank churns the water vigorously. This provides plenty of dissolved oxygen for these delicate baitfish. Shad tanks also are insulated to keep the water cool, but

Complete Angler's Library

it won't hurt to add some ice from time to time on hot days.

If you're using a shad tank, you must care for the shad while they're in the tank. Commercial chemicals are available, but two heaping handfuls of plain rock salt will meet most of the fish's needs. An anti-foaming agent keeps the shad's slime layer from creating a brown, scummy foam in the tank. Also, you will need a bait net for retrieving the shad from the tank. These nets are a 7- or 8-inch, fine-mesh basket with an 18- to 30-inch handle.

Incidental Gear

First and foremost, catfish anglers must have a large landing net. Choose a quality-made net with a large hoop, a stout yoke and a sturdy handle that will not bend when you try hoisting a 50-pounder into the boat. However, landing nets can disrupt the slime layer which covers the catfish's skin, leaving it prone to bacterial and fungal infections and parasitic infestations. Stiff, rough, monofilament nets also can damage the catfish's fragile skin. If you plan to release a catfish, do not use a landing net. Learn to "lip" cats just as you would when landing a bass; it is a snap once you get the hang of it. The catfish's lower jaw is similar to a suitcase handle, offering a perfect hand-hold.

A cutting board and a few fillet knives are a must. Also, take along a sharpener for the knives and your hooks. Sharp fillet knives will save you a lot of time in preparing cut bait. If you haven't already done so, stash a pair of needle-nose pliers and a pair of lineman's pliers in your boat or tackle box. They are invaluable for pulling hooks out of catfish or your buddy's finger.

Unless your boat has a giant livewell, you will need a big cooler or a long, heavy-duty stringer to hold cats that may run 30, 50 or 100 pounds.

Marker buoys come in handy to mark drop-offs, channel breaks, humps and holes. One company makes a lighted buoy that is powered by a single AA battery. Its soft, yellow glow is easily spotted several hundred yards away. Catfish anglers will find them helpful for those late-night outings under a dark moon. Also, these lighted buoys are great for marking trotline locations.

Rod Holders

The time-honored rod holder for bank anglers has been the forked stick. While there is no disputing the fact that they work,

A good, sturdy rod holder is an important piece of equipment on any catfishing boat. With rod holders, you can have several lines out and not worry about losing your equipment to a cat.

they leave something to be desired. The biggest problem is that a big cat will often take your equipment with him on his initial run. A third-world country could probably be run with the money squandered in equipment lost because of forked sticks. Nevertheless, forked sticks are a catfishing tradition.

In Europe, bank anglers use adjustable, metal rod holders so that poles can be positioned at various angles. Although these rigs are customarily used for carp, they work extremely well for catfish, too. Most often, the rod lays horizontally in the rod holder, parallel to the water. Sometimes, to minimize the wind effect on the line, the rodtip is pointed down at the water so that less line is in the air. In a river or stream where current plays with the line and makes strike detection a bit more difficult, the rod is pointed upward so that less line is in the water. These adjustable holders are available in the United States, but it may take some hunting to find one.

Several U.S. companies manufacture bank-type rod holders, most of which fit onto a long stake driven into the ground. Good ones allow you to make quick, easy, rod-angle adjustments.

If you fish from a boat, you will certainly want a few rod holders. Otherwise, you will be forced to hold your rod, limiting your fishing to just one or two lines. When drift fishing in a lake or large river, rod holders are a necessity. For an ideal setup, at least six sturdy rod holders would be placed in strategic locations around the boat. You might use 12 or more on larger boats.

Some models are attached to the boat with a small, unobtrusive plate mount. NAFC Members can buy a bunch of plate mounts for a couple of dollars each and position them around the boat so that a large number of rod holders won't be needed. Buy the minimum number of holders needed and use them wherever desired. Also, the rod holders can be removed when not needed, thus keeping them out of the way.

When purchasing rod holders, avoid those cheap, painted, pot-metal versions because they rust quickly and will not last through a season of hard use. Buy quality, well-constructed holders made of aluminum or stainless steel.

=======9=======

The Ideal Catfishing Boat

A merica's catfish anglers "get no respect." The fiberglass and graphite boys who chase largemouths and rub elbows with celebrity fishermen named Roland (Martin) and (Bill) Dance make fun of catfishermen, calling them "Bubba." The bassin' fraternity likes to joke that catfish anglers can't read well enough to learn to catch bass!

Catfishermen simply grin with a sly wink and, secure in the truth, they bask in the joshing attention given them. While bass anglers casting from $20,000 fishing platforms think they've done well to catch a few 12-inch fish, catfishermen are working from leaky flat bottoms which they would have trouble giving away ... and catching fish, as well. And, catfish anglers measure their fish in inches, too ... in inches between the eyes!

Catfish anglers look upon their boats as little more than tools used to get the job done. Catfish boats grow better with age, much like the well-worn, hickory-handled hammer that would not be traded for a dozen of those fancy models with fiberglass handles and cushioned grips. Every scratch is a story in itself. Every scrape a reminder of a special day gone by.

Today's catfishermen have several fishing crafts to choose from. Some work well in many different situations. Others are more specialized.

Canoe: Okay ... But

A good canoe will float in your yard after a summer rainstorm.

Catfisherman Tim Collett (seated) spends a lot of time on the water and his boat is outfitted with that thought in mind. It may not be fancy, the author says, but it is a reliable workhorse.

The Ideal Catfishing Boat 103

For this reason, canoes are often used in small streams where shallow sandbars may bring another craft to a screeching halt. These boats are light and, thus, easily carted down a creekbank or carried on a car top.

Most canoes range in size from 15 to 18 feet. They are available in either double-end (both ends pointed) or square-stern versions. Canoes can be propelled easily with a paddle—either upstream or down—and are surprisingly quick and extraordinarily agile. Fit an electric trolling motor or a tiny outboard to a square-stern canoe and you can motor effortlessly upstream.

Canoes are not very stable, however. Lean too far to one side and you are apt to get wet. For this reason, it is tough to fish for cats from a canoe. It takes some skill and dexterity to hoist a 30-pounder into a canoe without it keeling over.

For the catfish angler, canoes are best used for transportation between pools in small streams or rivers. At each shoal, tie the boat to a tree and wade around the holes. Fish the pool, hop back in the boat and head to the next one.

Johnboats: All-Around Choice

When most anglers think of a catfish boat, the image of a bruised-and-battered johnboat must certainly pop into their minds. And, rightly so, for no other single craft can meet the needs of so many catfish anglers.

Johnboats, originally designed for use in rivers, have wide, flat bottoms, providing a remarkable degree of stability. This makes them an ideal angling platform with a tremendous amount of open floor space. The johnboat's draft is so shallow that it can float in just a few inches of water. Johnboats are easily poled in the shallows; with a small outboard, you can go anywhere you want to go on a river, pond or small lake.

Although some homemade versions are constructed of marine-grade plywood with treated lumber supports, most commercial models are made of aluminum. A 12-foot aluminum model with a 52- to 56-inch beam can weigh as little as 120 pounds, making it an ideal car-topper. A boat of this size is easily toted up a riverbank and slipped into a small pickup's bed. A 5- to 10-horsepower outboard will make these little boats zoom.

Larger 14- to 20-foot models (too heavy to portage comfortably) can be customized to meet the needs of the most ardent cat-

A johnboat may be an NAFC Member's best choice for an all-round catfishing boat, providing you don't need to be on big, rough waters. It is the best shallow-draft boat around.

fish angler. Some come equipped with livewells and steering consoles. Floors can be decked or carpeted to reduce noise. Trolling motors can be attached to the bow or the stern, for drift fishing, and outboards in the 10- to 40-horsepower range provide all of the locomotion most small-water anglers will ever need.

Square-prowed johnboats with low freeboard height are unsuitable for rough water. They will not run well in choppy water, and large swells or waves may even capsize a smaller johnboat, particularly if the boat is caught sideways in the waves. Some newer johnboats have a modified v-hull. These will handle rough water better than the typical flat-bottomed version.

V-Hulls: Tops For Rough Water

V-hull and deep v-hulls have sharply pointed prows and relatively deep to very deep hulls, making them an ideal choice for rough water situations. The deep, pointed bows and v-shaped hulls of these boats cut through waves rather than riding over the top of them like a flat-bottomed johnboat. This provides a more stable, comfortable, safer ride.

V-hulls are available in many sizes, meeting virtually any need. Small 10- to 12-foot models are your basic, plain-Jane row boat; they are best fitted with a small outboard. Larger models, particularly those in the 16- to 20-foot range, are a much better choice for big-water angling and are the same type of boat commonly used by Great Lakes walleye anglers. Virtually all of the smaller v-hulls now produced are made with aluminum, while most larger models are fiberglass.

One drawback of a v-hull is the deep, sharply sloping sides resulting in a virtually unusable floor in the boat's bow section. A flat, albeit small, false floor is easily installed in the bow, and larger models often come fitted with complete, horizontal floors, running from bow to stern. In fact, many have all the comforts and amenities of the more luxurious bass boats.

Bass Boats/Catfish Boats

Bass boats aren't usually thought of as catfishing crafts, but they often serve that task admirably for anglers working larger rivers and impoundments. For covering a lot of water, hitting a lot of holes, in as short a time as possible, nothing beats a high-performance bass boat.

Their livewells, however, typically are too small for big cats, and there is usually not enough clear floor space for a shad tank. Also, most bass boat owners hate to see chicken livers, shad guts and congealed blood spilled on the nice, plush carpets. Other than those minor pitfalls, adding a few rod holders can turn a bass boat into a superb, comfortable catfishing craft for larger waters.

The Ultimate Catfishing Craft

For catfishing on our largest lakes, reservoirs and rivers, though, the finest boat is probably a craft typically referred to by freshwater anglers as a striper boat. These are large boats, measuring 18 to 22 feet or so, built upon a v-hull fiberglass or aluminum frame. For the most part, striper boats feature a center console design wherein the steering/throttle/electronics console is fitted into

Some fishermen call this boat a striper boat. It has a center console, allowing the catfisherman to walk around the perimeter and check the lines he has out.

the center of the boat's floor, resulting in a clear walkway all around the boat's perimeter. You have quick access to and from any part of the boat, a real asset when your reel's clicker is screaming and you are in the bow 15 feet away. Also, most of these boats have wide gunwales with plenty of mounting surface for rod holders, lantern holders, black lights or anything else you desire. Striper boats are roomy, safe, stable and quite comfortable. All things considered, they may be the ultimate catfishing boat for the big waters.

Customizing And Accessorizing

No matter what type of boat you fish from, a few accessories will enhance your enjoyment in using the craft and increase your angling productivity.

The Ideal Catfishing Boat

In most cases, an electric trolling motor is essential. It can be used to move the boat slowly while you're dragging baits over off-shore structure, particularly on those hot summer days when there is little wind to push the craft. Trolling motors also can be used to maintain direction and stay on a predetermined travel route when you're drifting, or when trying to present a bait with near surgical precision to an isolated depth break or some type of individual piece of structure.

In selecting an electric trolling motor, match the motor pow-er—rated in pounds of thrust—to the boat's size. For a smaller boat, a 12-volt motor, with about 18 to 28 pounds of thrust, may work well. Larger, heavier boats will need a 24-volt trolling motor which draws its power from two, 12-volt batteries and provides 25 to 45 pounds of thrust. Also, make sure you buy the correct shaft length for your craft. Large v-hulls require longer shaft lengths than typical johnboats or bass boats.

Some motors have foot controls so that the angler has both hands free for other tasks. Other models are steered by hand, with a continuous "power on" feature. This allows the angler to point the trolling motor in the desired direction. Choose the model you are most comfortable using.

No self-respecting catfish angler would leave the dock with-out a depthfinder. Most, in fact, have two or three on their boats. Selection is a very personal decision. If your boat has no console, sturdy clamp-on mounts are available for mounting your depth-finder (and a transducer) to the boat's side.

If you are an angler who habitually fishes large, expansive res-ervoirs, then you can benefit from having a Loran-C navigation device. These nifty devices allow you to return, within 50 to 100 feet or so, to a specific, precise location, by recording the coordi-nates, on virtually any body of water in the country.

Another must-have item on a catfishing boat is a set of quality rod holders. Depending on the boat's size, mount anywhere from four to 12, or even more, around the boat's perimeter. Because very few boats come equipped with a livewell large enough to han-dle even a moderate-sized catfish, you may want to add a large cooler (something in the 60- to 100-quart range) to your boat.

Catfish anglers need anchors, and you have two choices here: buy them or make them yourself. Store-bought anchors are prob-ably best because they hold your boat better than most homemade versions. However, they are expensive. Losing a few anchors each year puts a dent in your wallet.

Select an anchor designed for the type of bottom you will be over most often. Then, choose an anchor that is heavy enough to hold your boat. Obviously, larger boats require larger anchors. Danforth, or thin-fluked, anchors hold a boat over a sandy bottom. Navy-type, or heavy-fluked, anchors hold better on rocky bottoms. Mushroom anchors hold best in muddy bottoms, but are perhaps the best all-around anchor choice for most anglers.

Some anglers make their own anchors by filling large, plastic jugs with concrete or lead shot. A better homemade version can be made by poking a large, threaded eye-bolt through the side of a cardboard box, and then attaching a few large washers on the inside of the box with nuts. Next, tilt the box so the side with the bolt's eye is down. Fill it with concrete. When the cement hardens, you have a wedge-shaped anchor costing about one dollar that will hold tightly to the bottom.

Anglers fishing small rivers in small boats often use a drift anchor, which slows the boat's drift rather than holding it in place. A length of large, heavy chain or a couple of old window-sash-weights attached to a long rope will work. Anglers who drift with the wind on a large impoundment like to use a drift bag. These 2- to 4-foot-diameter, nylon bags serve as a brake, slowing the boat's drift. This allows your bait to remain on a structure a bit longer.

Your catfish boat is what you make of it. It can be as comfortable as a well-worn pair of blue jeans or as irritating as woolen underwear. Choose a craft that will best meet your needs. Don't compromise. Don't settle for the wrong boat simply because you find a bargain. Ultimately, it won't be such a bargain. Buy the right boat and then customize it to your liking. Take your time and outfit it a piece at a time. Eventually, your boat will reflect your own unique fishing style.

=10=

Catfish Baits: Good, Bad And Ugly

Catfish are omnivores, meaning they will eat almost anything. They function well as predators, and superbly as carrion salvagers. Catfish are also opportunistic feeders, meaning they eat whatever is available. Channel cats definitely are the most versatile feeders within the catfish family. They are equally adept at hunting live prey or locating a stinking mass a few hundred yards upriver. Blues tend to be more partial to live fish and crayfish, although they readily take cut bait, as well. Flatheads are piscivorous, meaning their overwhelming preference is live fish. Thus, the first step in selecting a catfish bait is determining which cats live in the waters you plan to fish.

Catfish guide, expert and national catfishing champion Ken Nelms says, "The best bait for catfish—and there are no ifs, ands or buts about it—is the natural forage that is most plentiful at any given time. Like all gamefish, cats get a kind of mind-set when they feed. If they've been eating shad and you offer them a shad, they'll jump all over your bait. But, if you offer them a pile of chicken livers, they might pass over that bait on their way to finding a shad to eat."

Those are words of wisdom (probably carved in stone somewhere). The next step is identifying the most commonly available natural forage. Figure that out and you are on your way to catching a lot of cats.

Try to collect natural bait, especially baitfish, near the waters

Shad are a prime live bait for catfish, particularly for flatheads and big blues. To keep them alive longer, hook them only through the upper lip; otherwise, they will suffocate.

Catfish Baits: Good, Bad And Ugly

you will be fishing. This assures that the bait is commonly available to the catfish you're after. It's even better to try to collect your baitfish from the waters or tributaries of the lake or river you will be fishing.

Catfish have an extraordinary sense of hearing. That, along with their lateral line system and vision, allows them to detect the struggles of a live baitfish even in off-colored water. Unless your baitfish is swimming or struggling, cats may have trouble locating it. It is wise, then, to keep a fresh, lively bait on your hook at all times. Remember, too, that cats can detect cut bait more easily than lifeless baitfish.

The catfish's super senses of smell and taste come into play when using cut bait (worms and such) or stinkbaits. It is important to remember that water current carries the bait's smell downstream. Your bait, then, should be presented either upstream of the feeding cats, or close to them.

One mistake fishermen commonly make is burying the hook's point in the bait. You will catch more fish if you leave the hook point exposed, especially when using a tougher offering like a whole, dead baitfish or a cut-bait strip. The bait often balls around the buried hook, keeping it from penetrating when the bait is in the catfish's mouth. It's better to leave the bait dangling in the hook's gap or bend. Don't worry about the exposed hook; the catfish won't!

Best Bets: Baitfish

Catfish probably feed more often on live or dead fish than on all other foods combined. Flatheads show a distinct preference for a diet of live fish. Blues, especially the larger specimens, prefer fish in their diet, too. But, unlike flatheads, blues will readily take a dead fish, or cut bait made from any kind of fish. And, channel cats? They're like Mikey; they'll eat anything!

The catfishermen who fish America's large rivers and expansive impoundments probably rely on members of the shad and herring families for most of their bait. These baitfish occur in numbers so large that they are the primary forage for the majority of predatorial fish. Most shad and herring are anadromous, living in saltwater and migrating into freshwater to spawn. Many populations became landlocked in dam impoundments. Those fish now live their entire lives as freshwater creatures. Others, like the

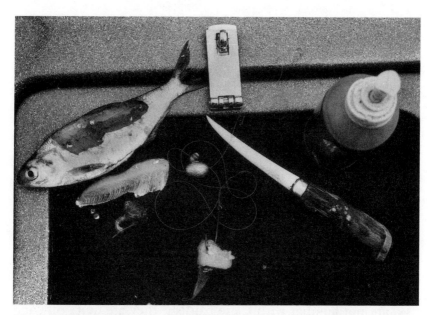

This photo shows the different ways that dead shad can be used as bait—either whole, filleted or cut into chunks. Even their entrails can be removed and wound onto a hook. The bait can be sprayed with attractant for added appeal.

blueback and skipjack herring, as well as the hickory shad, are still most commonly utilized during their migratory runs into freshwater where, for a time, they serve as the most abundant catfish forage around.

Gizzard shad, the most widespread species of the shad family, can be found virtually throughout the eastern two-thirds of the country. They are a favorite meal for the catfish, and, therefore, the catfish angler's favorite bait. Although gizzard shad can reach a length of about 20 inches, most measure 4 to 8 inches. A similar species, the threadfin shad, grows to a length of about 9 inches, although most are half that size or smaller. The Alabama shad is a favored baitfish along the Mississippi, Tennessee, Cumberland and Missouri rivers. The American shad, which is virtually identical to the Alabama shad, is popular on both coasts. Members of the herring family, primarily the skipjack and the blueback, are favorite baits of anglers looking for larger baitfish.

These baitfish travel in enormous schools, often congregating in the swift waters below dams. In those tailraces where shad congregate, they are the most prevalent food source for catfish. Also, shad are often swept from the main lake through the turbines. The wounded and ground-up baitfish exiting the turbine outflows are an easy meal for the big, lazy cats lying in wait.

In lakes and rivers, shad often travel near the surface, and the eagle-eyed angler can locate the schools by watching for their tell-tale "flips" or "spits" on the surface. They can be easily collected by throwing a circular cast-net that ensnares a number of the fish. Often, a single swirl of the net provides enough shad for an entire day's fishing.

Shad are difficult to use as a live bait because it is hard to keep them alive.

Hook a live shad or herring through the top lip or it will drown. These fish have very small mouths, and clamping the mouth shut with a hook will kill the bait almost as fast as if you stepped on it. As a rule, shad will not live very long when hooked, so check your bait often, replacing it with a fresh one periodically.

Shad and herring are, most often, used as a dead or cut bait. If you are not familiar with these baitfish, they are quite oily and smell ... well, really bad. Some catfishermen believe these qualities make the fish a productive cut bait because the shad's oil provides a strong scent trail that cats can easily locate and follow. Net some shad, toss them in a 5-gallon bucket with a few handfuls of ice and use them throughout the day or night. Dead shad can be utilized in several ways. By slitting the belly, you can easily remove the entrails (or guts) with your thumb and wind them on a 1/0 or 2/0 single hook or a small treble hook. Shad guts are extremely popular, being sold as a commercial bait along many catfish rivers. In faster-moving water, a shad fillet will stay on the hook quite well. Other anglers use a whole, dead shad, or portions of a larger shad, when hunting larger blue and channel cats. Ken Nelms, for example, prefers to cut a giant herring into four sections: the head, two gut/body sections and the tail, which he discards. His favorite bait is a hand-sized head from a big herring or a giant gizzard shad. (Make sure to match the size of your cut bait to the size of the catfish you expect to catch.)

In areas where shad and herring are not found, and in smaller streams and ponds, native minnows are the preferred live bait. Shiners, chubs, daces, fatheads and many others work well. These minnows can be collected in wire minnow traps that are baited with cornbread or biscuits. Bait the trap, drop it in a deep hole or pool and leave it overnight. Minnows are easily seined, too. And,

Complete Angler's Library

Using shad guts for bait can be somewhat messy, but it makes a superb bait, especially for small cats. (The small cats are quicker and outrun the big cats to the bait.)

when hooked through the back or lips, they are a hardy bait, as well.

Believe it or not, some well-versed catfish anglers believe that live goldfish are a superb bait, preferring them to all other minnows. In larger cities, goldfish can be purchased by the pound from bait houses and tropical fish supply stores. (Some states expressively prohibit the use of non-indigenous baitfish. So, be sure to check local game and fish regulations prior to using them because fines for these types of offenses are usually quite large.)

Those elite, catfish-fraternity members, who specialize in hunting monster cats, often prefer large, live baits. Carp in the 1- to 3-pound range are usually preferred, but suckers are popular, too. While that may seem large, remember that to a 90-pound cat, a 3-pound carp is nothing more than an appetizer. Live baits of this size are usually hooked through the back on a 6/0 to 10/0 hook and weighted with a slip sinker of up to ½ pound.

Carp and suckers also are commonly used as cut bait. Many anglers seem to prefer to use the flesh along the lower belly. Most fillet the fish, then cut the flesh into chunks or strips of the appropriate size. (Be sure to save the guts!) For smaller catfish, use strips about 1 inch wide and 3 inches in length. For larger fish, use proportionally larger cut-bait strips. Dedicated monster hunters often use a carp or sucker's entire side. Cut-bait strips should be rigged on a hook that is sized proportionally to the bait, with the hook remaining exposed.

During those hot summer days, when warm water can rapidly kill a hooked (and severely stressed) baitfish, live bluegill are a top choice. Bluegill are extremely hardy. Hooked through the lips or back, they will live for days on a hook. This also makes them a good choice when using a limbline, jug or trotline. (NAFC Members should check their state's game and fish laws before using any gamefish as bait. Often, bluegill taken by hook and line may be used as bait, but those captured with a net must be released immediately.) Use 2- to 3-inch bream for mid-sized cats and larger bluegill for the big cats.

Vigorous Victuals

Various natural baits are available to anglers, and catfish will eat all of them. Some, however, are better than others.

Nightcrawlers and redworms work great, especially in rivers and streams during the spring when crawlers are washed from their terrestrial haunts. The problem with worms, and all catch-all baits for that matter, is that other fish species often find them before the catfish do.

Although often considered the weekend catfisherman's bait, crawlers are often used by the experts with enormous success. Bob Holmes, a catfish guide and full-time outdoorsman from Trenton, Tennessee, often relies on nightcrawlers for many of his cat-catching chores. "Nightcrawlers are a convenience bait," he says. "But, catfish can't seem to get enough of them. When I am fishing to fill the freezer, I'm looking for cats in the 2- to 5-pound range, and nightcrawlers are one of the finest baits for these small fish. Occasionally, I'll catch a big cat on a worm, but most often it's the little ones that munch on crawlers."

While some experts lean toward shad or herring as the finest catfish bait, others prefer these catalpa worms. However, they are only available for a few weeks each summer.

Another worm considered superior to a crawler is the catalpa worm. In fact, some experienced catfish anglers say that catalpa worms are the best bait in the world for channel cats! That may be true, but obtaining enough of these black and yellow worms is difficult. They are only found in catalpa trees for a few weeks during the summer.

Holmes relies heavily on catalpa worms so he has developed a way to preserve them for future use. "After collecting a batch of catalpa worms," he says, "I'll put them in boiling water for 15 or 20 seconds, let them cool and then freeze them in water. This helps retain their texture and color."

Another worm that should not be overlooked is the green worm, an olive-colored, foul-smelling creature that can often be found in the more undesirable places along sandy riverbanks. An-

If gamefish could vote on popular baits, they would probably vote for the crayfish. They can be used live or dead. Just peel the white meat out of the tail and slip it on the hook.

other terribly underrated catfish bait is big grasshoppers. In late summer, when hordes of these insects have reached a length of several inches, they become particularly effective when fished in smaller streams. Rig them on a light wire hook and drift them through fast-moving riffles and into the quiet pools below. Likewise, locusts (cicadas) work great when used in a similar way. Problem is, they are only available every 17 years!

Frogs and tadpoles, although not common cat baits, have their following. Bullfrogs are usually killed prior to use and the legs saved for the skillet! Large, live bullfrog tadpoles are an ignored, but effective bait. Once dead, however, these soft-bodied larvae decompose rapidly, so they are not a good choice for limbline or trotline use.

If you can keep the smallmouth bass away, live crayfish are

superb catfish baits. When hooked through the tail, both hard- and soft-shelled crayfish produce. Also, the skinned out, white-meat tail portions by themselves are a truly fabulous bait, although many anglers prefer to eat those themselves. Blue cats, in particular, have a definite affinity for crayfish.

Many old-time anglers like using clam and mussel meat as bait. These bivalve mollusks have, however, become difficult to obtain and do not seem to be any better as bait than the easier-to-catch natural baits. (Clams and mussels are a protected species in some states. Check your local regulations before capturing them.) To make these baits smell more, some anglers soak the inside meaty portions of the shellfish in sour milk for a few days before using them.

In coastal rivers and tidal streams, many types of brackish and saltwater crustaceans are superb catfish baits. Shrimp are extremely popular, as are both hard- and soft-shelled crabs. Glenn Peacock, a guide from Silver Spring, Maryland, who catfishes in the Potomac River, has found hard-shelled crabs to be a more productive catfish bait than the commonly used soft-shelled ones.

From shad to shiners and crabs to crawlers, the number of natural baits that catfish will eat is almost as high as the number of stars in the sky on a clear winter's night. Pick the right one and put it in the right place and you will get your line stretched!

11

Stinkbaits: Odoriferous Offerings

Stinkbaits are best utilized in early spring. Creatures that perished during the winter decompose only slightly in the cold, icy waters. Once the water begins to warm, however, decomposition proceeds rapidly. Catfish, therefore, probably feed more often on rotting carrion in the early spring than at any other time. Because cats follow scent trails and feed on rank, smelly, putrid objects in the early weeks of spring, anglers can often gain an advantage using a similar offering that is impaled on a hook.

That is not to say, however, that stinkbaits are not productive throughout the year.

Stinkbaits, Brews And Concoctions

The most convenient catfish baits are those ready-to-fish baits that a number of manufacturers produce. They certainly are not natural to the catfish, and they rarely out-produce live or cut baits. But, they are, nevertheless, productive at times. For the most part, baits of this type seem to catch smaller cats. If you seek big cats, use big, natural baits.

All of the dough or tub-type stinkbaits can be molded into dough balls around a hook. Treble hooks fitted with a wire coil around the shank are designed to hold these pastes. Then, there are dough worms—plastic, worm-type baits with molded grooves which firmly hold a dough bait. A monofilament leader, tied to the main line, runs through the worm and ties to a treble hook at

Stinkbaits work especially well for the smaller catfish, but are a popular producer of good-sized cats especially during early spring. These baits are popular for night-fishing because the catfish's sense of smell is so keen.

Stinkbaits: Odoriferous Offerings

the worm's base. Finally, a small sponge square can be cut, fitted over a treble hook's shank and rolled in the bait.

For those who don't want to touch foul-smelling potions, tube baits are the ticket. These paste-baits are packaged in squeeze tubes, to be used with hollow plastic catfish "tube-lures." To use, simply insert the tube's spout into the lure's slit and fill it by squeezing the tube. In water, the bait slowly dissolves, oozing out of the lure's "vapor holes," hopefully attracting a hungry catfish. While commercially produced catfish tube-lures are available, they are fairly expensive. Homemade versions can be made using a bass angler's hollow tube-lure and a treble hook. They are cheaper, and work just as well.

The weekend catfish angler's favorite bait probably is chicken livers. Because they are cheap, convenient, bloody and quite productive, chicken livers will remain the favorite bait of many casual catfishermen, even though they might not be the most productive bait.

Chicken livers can be rather difficult to keep on the hook. To solve this problem, use a small treble hook and push the hook's shank through the liver's center, impaling each of the three hook points into the liver. Another solution is to leave a 5- or 6-inch length of excess line when tying your hook to the main line. Then, use this tag to bind the liver to the hook. A better method, however, is securing the liver in a small pouch made from 3- or 4-inch-square pieces of discarded nylon stocking. Such a pouch made from the hosiery is porous and tough. It allows all of the tantalizing scents and juices to ooze out into the water while preventing a little bait-stealer from robbing you blind.

Beef liver, also an effective, easy-to-use and easy-to-obtain catfish bait, can be found in your grocer's meat cooler. These large livers are usually purchased in slices. Cut them into strips or squares and drop them into a pot of boiling water for just a minute or two. This will toughen the liver so it will stay on a hook.

Although offensive to the weak stomach, the entrails of various creatures often are good baits. As already discussed, shad entrails are a great bait. Chicken entrails are good, as well, and can be easily obtained (usually at no charge) at any chicken farm or processing plant. Wrapped around a treble hook or packed in a hose-bag, they can be drifted through riffles or still-fished with a slip-sinker rig in deeper pools.

Homemade Tube Lure

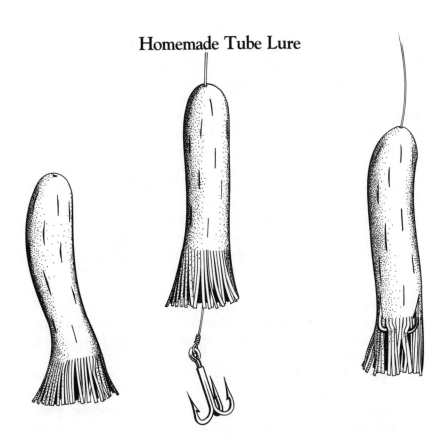

This homemade tube lure is built using a bass angler's tube lure. The tube is slit, allowing scented bait to drift out. An appropriate-sized treble hook is added to complete the rig.

If you happen to be timid and afraid of getting your hands dirty or smelly, you may want to try Ivory soap. That's right, plain, old Ivory soap! To use, simply cut an Ivory soap bar into small cubes, bore a hole through the center and slide the hook's shank through the hole prior to tying it to your line. Another tasteful option for the weak stomach is Spam or Treet luncheon meat, or pieces of strong cheese like limburger, garlic or sharp cheddar. Cut any of the above into ½- to 1-inch cubes and slip it on your hook.

Home-Brews And Baits

Despite the glut of commercially prepared stinkbaits available to today's catfish angler, many prefer to brew their own. Favorite recipes and potent potions proven to produce, have been passed on through generations. Homemade catfish baits, like faded blue jeans and good apple pie, are an American tradition. And, traditions die hard in this great country. You might want to try one of the following recipes. All have been used successfully for decades:

The Super-Stink Sponge-Bait Special: Place several dozen small minnows, a few sliced shad, or several carp fillets into a wide-mouthed jar. Put the jar on the sunniest portion of your roof for a few days while the fish parts decompose. When only an oily liquid remains, the potion is ready. Next, cut a sponge into 1-inch cubes and drop the cubes into the jar. Screw the lid on tightly, shake the jar for a few minutes and let the sponges soak in the solution until ready to use. When fishing, pull a sponge from the liquid with a stick or a pair of pliers and place it on your hook. The liquid will slowly dissipate from the sponge, so you should replace it with a fresh one about every 30 minutes. Drop the old sponge back into the jar for later use.

A Cheese-Burger (that only a catfish could love!): Mix equal portions of raw, ground hamburger (fish can also be used) and a strong, grated cheese such as limburger. Add a little hot water and mix thoroughly with your hands. Now, work just enough flour into the paste to make the bait stick together. (Some anglers add cotton or gauze to help hold the bait together.) Form the dough into balls of the appropriate size, drop them into a sealable, plastic bag and refrigerate until ready to use.

Cheese-Its: Simply mix ½ pound strong, finely grated cheese with 4 cups flour. Add just enough water to stiffen the dough. If desired, a few teaspoons of anise oil, vanilla extract, an angling scent or any other possible attractant may be added. Form the dough into balls of the desired size and let dry (outside) for one or two hours. Next, drop the doughballs into boiling water and cook for about 30 minutes. Then, remove them and let dry. Store in a sealable, plastic bag in the refrigerator until ready to use.

Honest-To-Goodness Blood Bait

Catfish guide Bob Fincher has no trouble picking his favorite catfish bait. "Blood!" says Fincher. "Blood contains nature's strongest odors to a predator, and catfish are true predators that feed most of the time by smell. The smell of blood signals an easy meal for a catfish, and sends them into a feeding frenzy just like sharks. I reckon I've been using blood for about 25 years now, and there's not a bait in the world that will catch more catfish."

Blood is a popular additive for many of the prepared baits because it attracts cats. But, even cheese is popular on the catfish menu. Catfishermen have a wide choice of prepared baits.

Fincher developed his own blood bait through several years of research and markets it via mail order as "Bob's Secret Formula Pure Chicken Blood Catfish Bait." Lots of stinkbaits advertise a blood additive, but some say that Bob's congealed blood is the only true blood bait in the country. Fincher collects the crimson liquid from a chicken processing plant and treats it with salt (forcing water out of the clot) and a food preservative. "Other than those two additives," he says, "my bait is 100 percent pure chicken blood."

Unlike most stinkbaits, true blood produces catfish consistently year-round. From the dead of winter to the dog days of August, blood will call the cats to the dinner table.

Congealed blood is squishy, soft and obviously messy. "If that bothers you," Bob says, "you need to take up knittin' or golf!" He recommends keeping a pail of rinse water in the boat for a quick hand-washing after baiting your hooks. This clotted blood is odorless to humans.

Because this bait is soft and easily lost or stolen from the hook, it must be rigged properly to remain effective. For most of his blood-fishing trips, Fincher uses a special two-hook rig. When the rig is in use, the hooks dangle from the loop's bottom.

To bait the rig, pinch off a piece of blood about the size of a silver dollar, fold it like a taco and push the hooks through both folds of the blood clot. When rigged correctly, most of the blood clot is cradled in the bends of the hooks. The hosiery-bag rig works well, too. The blood clots can also be cut into strips and wound around the hook's shank. To further reduce the chance of flinging the clotted blood into space, Fincher recommends using spincast or spinning gear and making short, lob-casts.

Good Scents, Or Nonsense?

When angling scents first appeared, they took the market by storm. That worm-flippin', bass bunch embraced the concept with open arms, and the jig-dunkin', crappie fanatics weren't far behind. But, this was far from new to the catfish addicts—those gentle souls who had been mixing secret potions for decades. A little anise oil dribbled on a bait has often been credited with calling cats over from the next county. Rhodium oil might remind you of a rose garden, but some still swear that it brings cats racing to a bait. Vanilla extract smells wonderful, and some experts believe cats find it as pleasing as we do. WD-40, a water-displacing lubricant often used by outdoorsmen, has been sprayed on baits for years. Some high-brows laughed … until they learned that a principal ingredient of the lubricant is a mixture of fish emulsions, or fish oils.

Given the catfish's phenomenal sense of smell, there is no doubt that a scent additive can be attractive to them, and thus helpful to the angler. The key, however, is selecting a scent that appeals to catfish. A smell that catfish associate with a food source is certainly more appealing, and will be much more apt to attract a cat. Obviously, blood and bodily juices of dead and dying baitfish are extremely attractive to these whiskered fiends and provide the finest scent trail of all.

Several other catfishing scents are also available. Some are claimed to "strategically disperse" in the water (read that as "dissolve in water"). Others are said to provide a direct pathway to your bait (read that as "drift downstream"). Others contain pheromones and various secret chemicals that supposedly excite fish and stimulate a feeding response. And, believe it or not, one popular fishing scent was originally made from grill drippings after a cook-out!

Some catfish anglers are convinced that certain commercially-prepared angling scents are indeed very beneficial, especially when used with dry baits. Others prefer to stick with those "tried-and-true" cut baits that exude nature's own version of an angling scent. Nevertheless, these scent additives are worth a try. Even if the application does nothing more than increase your confidence in the bait, it is worth using.

A Convincing Case For Chum

Long regarded as a tactic solely for attracting sharks in saltwater, chumming is also highly effective for catfishing. Bob Fincher ranks chumming as the single, most important tactic any catfish angler can learn. "It is the easiest way to insure your success when catfishing," he says, emphatically.

In simplest terms, chumming puts material into the water that exudes a scent and attracts fish. Chumming is a superb tactic when you regularly fish favorite water holes. Best results occur after you've baited a hole for several consecutive days prior to fishing because a continuous flow of scent will keep cats—maybe not the same cats—coming to check out this potential food source. The easiest way to chum is with a burlap or cheese-cloth sack attached with string to a tree near your fishing hole. Every few days, simply refill the bag with bait, drop in a rock for weight and toss the sack back into the water.

It is important not to feed the cats too much, but to tease, tantalize and keep them coming back for more to eat. A skilled chum-slinger can keep cats hanging around, anxiously anticipating an easy meal, much like teenage boys who cruise the local fast-food joints night after night.

Many things can be used as chum. Fincher produces a commercially-prepared chum made from congealed chicken blood which is forced through a fine-mesh screen; the pellets (or giblets, as he calls them) are small, barely enough for the cats to

Effective chumming can produce good results. The secret is to tease the cats with small amounts of chum in order to keep them coming back. Don't overfeed them.

Complete Angler's Library

eat, but still effective. Cheap dog and cat food will bring catfish to your bait, as will ground or minced minnows, carp or shad.

Some anglers, believe it or not, chum with road kill! One angler from Georgia carries a supply of burlap bags and a coal shovel in his rusty pickup. Whenever he sees a dead animal on the road, he stops and scoops it up, and tosses it in a burlap sack along with a few fist-sized rocks. He then ties a rope to the bag, attaches the rope to a tree and tosses it into one of his favorite fishing holes. A day or two later, he will either drop a fish trap into the hole or scour it with a baited hook. Does it work? Well, some believe this angler's crooked back resulted from years of toting monster cats up the creekbank.

Soybean cakes, hay bales and cracked corn attract minnows and baitfish to an area, which in turn attract predatory fish. However, smelly—particularly bloody—conglomerations attract catfish much better. Catfish have the finest noses in freshwater; use that fact to increase your odds of success.

Locating Cats

12

Fishing Small Streams, Rivers

C atfish evolved in this country as a river fish. From Kansas' farm-country creeks to the mountain streams of the Appalachians, catfish reign as king. Despite the overwhelming popularity of the impoundments scattered across America, the majority of catfishing—both recreational and commercial—occurs in streams and rivers.

Anatomy Of A River

From the tiniest mountain stream to the largest flathead river, all moving bodies of water share the same basic anatomy. Many people look at a river and see a chaotic, haphazard array of bottom conditions and water depths. Knowledgeable anglers, however, know a river's framework follows a predictable pattern, a pattern that, once learned, provides key insights into locating catfish.

First of all, remember that water flow is one of nature's most powerful forces. One glance at the Grand Canyon confirms that fact. This giant gorge, carved by the Colorado River over millions of years, is some 217 miles long and up to a mile deep. The Mississippi River's enormous water flow, averaging some 1,640,000 cubic feet per second, wreaks havoc upon the river's underlying strata. In fact, the monstrous Mississippi changes its course so often that its length varies some 40 to 50 miles each year. Although most of our rivers and streams are more tame, rivers are *not* static.

Rivers are nothing more than water flowing over the terrain. Over time, the water current digs a channel, washing away softer

When fishing small rivers, you should learn to identify quickly the shoal-hole-flat sequence. This angler is fishing the front edge of a hole that was formed below this shoal.

Fishing Small Streams, Rivers   133

soil and depositing it downstream. Hard, rocky areas maintain their integrity against the force of the water's flow. These factors combine to create the river anatomy that successful catfish anglers have learned to read and understand.

A river can be divided effectively into three water types: pools, shoals and flats. Pools represent the deepest water in the river. Shoals are swift, shallow water, often called rapids or riffles. Flats are long stretches of water characterized by a relatively level, smooth, unchanging bottom and constant depth. Pools, shoals and flats occur in predictable patterns. Typically, a shoal is at the beginning of the sequence, followed by a pool and then a flat. In essence, a river is a reoccurring pattern of shoals, pools and flats.

Shoals occur over hard, rocky terrain not easily moved by the water's flow. The carrying capacity, or the amount of water flowing through an area, decreases at a shoal. This constriction generates increased water pressure in front of the shoal and forces the water to rush rapidly forward over the constricted areas—the shoal's hard, shallow bottom. In smaller streams, particularly where the water's path is narrow such as in a canyon, shoals span the water from bank to bank. Move over to a larger stream or a mid-sized river and shoals may only span only a portion of the river's channel. Nonetheless, there still will be a hole downstream from the shoals.

Shoals end where hard, rocky bottoms turn into softer soil. Water rushing forward dislodges the soil, creating a pool. These pools are the deepest holes in the river, serving as activity centers for both catfish and anglers.

The current's force at the hole's downstream edge is still strong, carrying the dislodged soil downstream. As the river gradually grows wider, the current moderates. Soil settles to the bottom, creating a flat. When the river widens rapidly after a shoal, flats or smaller pools start to form around the larger pool at the shoal's base.

Not all rivers are good catfish rivers. The clear, cool, shallow mountain brook racing downstream over a rocky substrate may be an ideal habitat for trout, but catfish don't like it. Cats prefer warmer, slower-moving streams that are deeper and more turbid. Catfish often begin showing up in the middle stretches where the river's gradient decreases, and depth begins to increase. Tributaries flowing into the river add to its depth, while often providing a

In this quiet bank-fishing scene, the major decision is determining where the force of the main current has deepened the channel. The cats will be in the deepest water.

larger forage base and added fertility. In a trout stream, shoals tend to be the brook's longest sections. In a good catfish river, shoals are the shortest sections and flats the longest.

Learning to "read" the river by studying the water and its flow and then visualizing the structure underneath, is perhaps the most important task for any river angler. In streams and small rivers, it is not at all difficult. The shoal-pool-flat sequence usually is obvious. Shoals can be spotted easily from a distance by simply looking for the riffled surface. Pools naturally follow shoals. Flats often appear glassy-smooth, unless some underlying structure is disturbing the surface current.

Locating Catfish

The center of a river cat's universe is the pool. Catfish inhabit

"Shoal-Pool-Flats" Sequence

This drawing illustrates the shoal-hole-flat sequence. The downward force of water tumbling over the shoals creates a depression just beyond the shoal, and that's where you'll find the cats.

these holes throughout the year except while spawning. They eat, rest and spend their lives in these deep pools. Water racing across the hard, rocky bottom of the upstream shoal is well-oxygenated. Cats like that. At night, lower air temperatures cool the water as it flows in a thin layer over the rocks. Cats like that, too.

Catfish, in a sense, are deep-water fish. Given a choice, they will opt for a deep hole rather than a shallow one. Deep pools offer safety, shelter and comfort.

Cats choose pools because foraging is easier there. Lying in the pool below a shoal, cats can see, smell, taste or feel virtually all food that is washed downstream. Shoals are terrific homes for insects and crustaceans, many of which are swept from their rocky crevices into the pool below. Cats learn this at an early age and capitalize on it throughout their lives.

Some pools are better than others. The largest, deepest pools almost always hold cats. Add some structure and the pool becomes nearly a sure-thing. Structure is important, especially for big cats. A few big rocks at the pool's head break the current; cats will lie in wait in the quiet water behind them, ready to ambush anything. An old tree that lodges in the pool will attract and hold the cats.

Catfish location is a dynamic process. Periods of high water will have cats roaming out beyond their pools. They will eventually take up residence in another hole. Good pools, however, always hold fish. Many rivers have community holes—pools of water that every local angler knows about and everyone visits. While these pools may produce fish from time to time, NAFC Members can certainly increase their chances for success by scouting out a few new, less-known holes.

Actively feeding cats typically will gather at the pool's upstream edge, just below the shoal. Some venture into the shoal itself; young flatheads often do at night. Smaller cats may make brief excursions onto the flats at the other end of the hole, but larger fish usually remain in the pool. Cats will jockey for position in the hole, with the larger, more-dominant individuals taking the choice spots. While the pool's forward edge attracts the most active feeders, the rear portion becomes a catfish sanctuary. The deeper water offers security, and the current is slight, so the fish can rest. That is not to say, however, that cats do not feed in the pool's tail-end, because they often do.

Most often, flats are not important to the catfish angler. A piece of structure breaking the current might be worth fishing for a minute or two, but if it only produces a lone whiskerface that lost its way, move on. You will not find many cats, nor will you find large cats, in a river flat. Catfish use flats rarely, so hurry through them. Spend your time more productively fishing the different pools.

Another deep-water haunt historically ranking on a par with a pool is a river bend's outside edge. The deepest portion of any river bend is along its outside edge where current is strongest. The strong current erodes the bottom, preventing silt from settling, and thus creating a deep-water stretch. Silt accumulates along the bend's inside edge where current is weak, so this area is normally shallower than the outside edge.

Like pools, river bends provide a deep-water sanctuary for the cats. The direct current flow into the outside bank makes easier feeding for cats. Although they are not lazy fish, cats know that if they position themselves in the right places, the current will bring the food to them. Feeding cats typically position themselves in the forward, or upstream, section of the river bend near the outside channel bank. Inactive cats will usually remain in the deeper water along the bend's outer edge; however, they often hold near the end of the bend where the current is not quite as strong. Again, any type of structure—fallen trees, large rocks, man-made objects—in the river bend will cause the fish to congregate.

Tributaries and feeder creeks usually increase a river's overall fishing productivity. The water stretch just downstream from the creek's mouth may be a hole, especially if the creek is relatively large or fast-flowing. More often than not, however, the stretch just below the creek mouth will be shallow from siltation, particularly if the creek drains an agricultural area, or other high-soil erosion areas. Over time, many creeks deposit rocks and gravel at their mouths, forming sandbars which may stretch well out into the main stream. Eventually, the stream flow constricts; a shoal or riffled area develops, and a pool forms below the shoal. Large pools that are fed by a creek are likely hotspots for catfishermen.

Catfishing In Small To Mid-Sized Rivers

When NAFC Members fish anything from a small stream to a mid-sized river, their best strategy often will be a hit-and-run approach. Pools tend to be small, and there won't be an abundance of cats in any one hole. Read the river. Keep moving. If a hole produces, stick with it. If not, move on.

If the river is shallow enough, wading is a great tactic. You might want to use a canoe or small flat-bottomed boat to cruise rapidly over the flats, stopping to wade around the shoals and pools. When not confined to a boat, you can make your way to ideal vantage points and work the pools in a precise, methodical manner. An old fly-fishing vest is a much needed accessory when wading; its many pockets provide places for a box of hooks, a little bag of split shots, a few bobbers, pliers, a stringer and even some of your chosen bait.

River cats pounce on moving forage. Baitfish swim, crayfish scuttle and the current washes everything downstream. Why, then, do some anglers limit themselves by slipping a heavy sinker onto the line and anchoring the bait in one place? Tradition, perhaps—who knows.

Catfish anglers can dramatically increase their productivity when drifting their baits through a river's pools and current chutes. You can cover more water, fish a lot faster, catch many more fish and have more fun, as well.

Just because the water is shallow doesn't mean you won't find catfish there. Wading the shallows can be more effective than working them from a boat. Some anglers use a boat only for transportation from hole to hole.

Put on enough weight to get the bait down to the catfish; yet, not enough so the offering drifts unnaturally or drops to the bottom and stays there. Using relatively short leaders, or keeping the distance between the sinkers and the hook short, insures that the bait is pulled down into the pool rather than drifting over the heads of catfish. The following terminal tackle rigs function effectively in the search for river cats.

The basic split-shot rig works well and probably is used more often than any other stream rig. It does, however, have some limitations. Split shots crimped onto the main line often weaken it. If the shots snag, they will slide along the line, often abrading it. Also, if the shots snag, your efforts to free the rig often pull the hook and bait over to the snag, making matters worse.

The basic steelhead rig works in those coastal rivers where

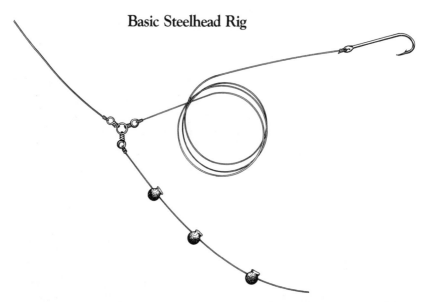

Basic Steelhead Rig

Catfishermen aren't fussy. They'll use whatever works including this basic steelhead rig with split shots added to the dropper. Enough shot should be added so the rig will bump the bottom, but not enough to hang up.

steelheads make their spawning runs and also functions extraordinarily well as a rig for stream-bound catfish. The split shots crimped onto the short dropper line will simply slide off the line if they become snagged. Anglers adding or removing split shots can do so without fear of weakening the main line. A short leader of heavier test line can be used with the three-way swivel to safeguard against the main line being abraded from the cat's sandpaper-like teeth. The steelhead rig probably is the best all-around choice for drifting baits through a catfish stream.

The pencil-sinker rig is a spin-off of the steelhead rig. The only difference between the two is the addition of a short piece of rubber or surgical tubing to the short dropper line. When a pencil-lead sinker is inserted into the tubing, this rig becomes one of the most snag-resistant setups known to catfish (and steelhead) anglers. And, should the sinker snag, a tug on the line will slip it out of the tubing.

When you're fishing a relatively shallow stream on a mild to moderate gradient, a bobber or float may be needed. When used correctly, floats often provide a more natural bait presentation to the catfish. The bait moves naturally downstream, responding to

Pencil-Sinker Rig

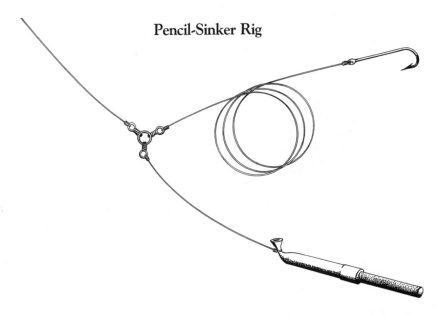

If you're catching more snags—particularly on rocky bottoms—than fish, the pencil-lead rig is worth a try. If the weight snags, all you lose is the pencil-lead weight.

the current, flowing through chutes, skirting around rocks and settling enticingly in pools. Floats are often the only way to fully work the circular currents that occur behind large rocks, fallen trees and other current breaks. These currents tend to be rather mild, and a split-shot rig will simply settle to the bottom. However, a float rig will drift with the currents, covering the water thoroughly.

Those popular red-and-white round plastic bobbers will work for catching catfish, but balsa-wood floats are a better choice. Those that are shaped much like a kid's toy top are probably the best choice for most situations. They will support a heavy piece of cut bait, but even with a lighter offering, they ride lower in the water than a plastic ball. Thus, they aren't tossed around quite so much from currents. As a general rule, floats are valuable when the water is not deeper than 8 feet or so. In shallower water—6 feet or less—float rigs probably surpass drift rigs in overall effectiveness, ease of use and fishing enjoyment.

Although many floats are simply clipped in place on the line, this type of rig can be awkward and cumbersome to cast. A better setup is the slip-float rig. The float slides freely on the line. A stop-

Slip-Float Rig

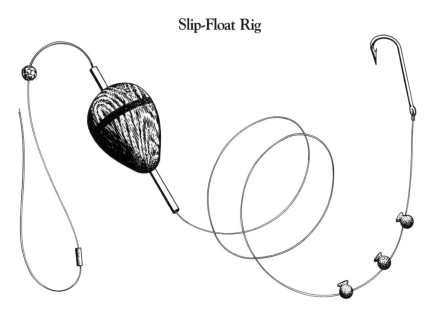

Another catfish rig that panfishermen would recognize is this slip-float rig. An oval, balsa float works best, and you add just enough split shot to keep your bait close to the bottom.

knot tied on the line or a commercially made bobber-stop snapped in place on the main line, stops the float which supports the bait at the desired depth. Usually, a small plastic bead separates the float and the bobber-stop, preventing the stop from wedging in the bobber's mouth or spout. The float, then, is allowed to slide on the line between the sinkers and the bobber-stop.

When you're preparing to cast, the bobber-stop can be reeled in through the rod's guides, leaving just a short piece of main line with the bobber, sinkers and hook dangling from the rodtip. Casting is easy. When this rig hits the water, the sinkers pull the line through the float until it hits the bobber-stop.

In all but the slowest currents, the split-shot sinkers crimped onto the line below the bobber should be about 4 to 6 inches apart from each other, starting about 12 inches or so above the hook. This makes the line arc in the water so the float actually leads the bait downstream. Drifts like this are more natural, and the rig will not snag so easily. The amount of weight you use depends on the current's force. Rather than choosing one large split shot, use three smaller ones and spread them on the line about 6 inches apart with the lower-most shot spaced 6 inches above the hook.

To achieve a good, natural drift, keep your line off the water's surface. The current pulls the line laying on the water, creating a bow in the line. When this happens, the float or bait is pulled across the current. Ultimately, this causes the bait to move unnaturally through the water. Feeding chutes are missed, pools are bypassed and fish are lost. Long rods which can bring the line high off the water are your best defense, and taking an active role in the drift—releasing line and retrieving slack at the appropriate moments—is vital, too.

In most instances, drift fishing works best when you cast slightly upstream; then, allow the bait and rig to drift downstream with the current. Keep your rod up, your line out of the water and your eye on the float. If you are not using a float, watch the line at the point where it enters the water.

Maintaining a tight line is critical when stream fishing. If the line has some slack, it will bow downstream ahead of the bait. Unless you use a float, you will never feel the fish hit. And, even with a float, you are not in a good position to set the hook. Jerking all of the slack line out of the water leaves no force in the rod's swing to drive the hook home in the catfish.

=========13=========

Fishing Larger Rivers

merica's big rivers share the same anatomy as smaller creeks and streams, but on a much larger scale. Giant rivers like the Mississippi, Ohio and Missouri, as well as their larger tributaries, all have the same recurring pattern of shoals, pools and flats. These areas, however, are not as easily located in a big river as they are in a stream. The enormous water flow and substantial average depths camouflage these underwater formations, thus making scouting for good fishing spots a bit more difficult.

Those difficulties, however, are not without reward. Big rivers have an enormous forage base for cats. Food is plentiful, life is easy and catfish grow big and mean. Larger waters support larger fish populations, so cats are not in short supply.

Scouting Big Rivers

In smaller rivers and streams, a well-versed angler can glance at the water's surface and know instantly what structure lies below. Shoals are evidenced by rough, rapid water. Pools occur below shoals, although no surface commotion signals their presence. And, flats typically house slick water that is broken only by the occasional snag or rock on an otherwise flat bottom.

These same structures occur in big rivers, but the enormously wide and deep waters often give no hint as to the structure lying below. Occasionally, the surface may be roiled by a shallow shoal or a wing dam, but, for the most part, anglers will be forced to use

144   Complete Angler's Library

Big rivers can mean big cats. This is one morning's catch for catfisherman Tim Collett. The biggest blue weighed in at 30 pounds; and, he caught one flathead weighing 20 pounds.

Fishing Larger Rivers 145

another set of eyes—the depthfinder—when hunting productive catfish structure.

Larger rivers often pose an added hindrance to an angler's scouting efforts. Dams and locks created along the river raise the overall water level, concealing the original river channel under a wide sea of flat, moving water. The original channel will usually be bordered on either side by a relatively level flat. The best catfishing structure typically centers around the old channel. The flats may hold roaming cats, but the holes, pools and deep-water sanctuaries in and adjacent to the channel hold vast numbers of catfish. Thus, the first step in scouting a river is defining the original channel. Often, if the river is navigable, looking for the navigation buoys will accomplish that task for you.

Catfish utilize the same types of structure in both small streams and big rivers. Typically, pools or holes and the river bend's outside edges hold the largest catfish populations. Old, now-submerged dams and locks, wing dams and shallower shoals will all signal a hole below them. Sudden changes in depth and current breaks created from solid structure (wing dams, rock piles and bridge pilings) are prime feeding locations. Most knowledgeable anglers consider the edges between swift and mild current flows to be key points within these areas. As a general rule, the current positions the catfish in predictable locations. Feeding cats often lurk behind a current break, lying in wait to ambush some critter. Catfish seem to face into the current, but that is not always upstream. Currents zig and zag around structure, sometimes flowing across the river and occasionally up the river in an eddy-type situation.

In larger rivers, the increased average depth lets catfish roam a bit more than they do in a stream, although most movements are still between deeper water holes. Blue cats are notorious ramblers. They often travel in packs, and move together onto feeding structure. Channel cats and flatheads roam as well, but not to the same extent as blues.

Hunting catfish-holding structure in a large river is best accomplished with an outboard-equipped boat and a depthfinder. A vast amount of water can be covered—and the bottom studied—if an angler moves slowly while watching the depthfinder. Flashers work well in defining underwater structure while moving. Liquid crystal units do, too, but because they keep the image on the

Rock bluffs and river bends spell catfish. These holes provide good catfishing on most big rivers. Drift fishing is usually the most productive method because you can cover a lot of water.

screen quite a bit longer, many anglers prefer them for this type of scouting. Paper graphs work well, but are expensive to operate for extended time periods. Use a flasher or liquid crystal unit for scouting, then switch to the paper graph to study the structure and the fish holding on it.

Because many large rivers are impounded at intervals by large dams with giant reservoirs behind them, their flow is often regulated. Small dams raise rivers only slightly, and lock systems assist in nautical traffic and navigation. Downstream currents depend upon the water being released from an upstream and/or a downstream dam. Sometimes, the currents rage downstream. Sometimes, the river barely has a perceptible current. Usually, the flow is rather stable with periodic increases in current that result primarily from hydroelectric generating facilities.

Peak catfish feeding periods often tie to these changes in current flow. Whenever additional water is released from the dam, catfish tend to feed. This is most evident on rivers located below a dam fitted with a hydroelectric generating plant. The generating schedule regulates these river currents. The catfish's peak feeding periods coincide with the increased water flow, regardless of the time of day. Cats don't always prowl at night.

Covering Deep River Holes

Tillman "Tim" Collett is something of a catfish virtuoso. A native of Lenoir City, Tennessee, he pursues catfish virtually every day along the Tennessee River.

"Deep river holes are the best areas that I have found for consistently producing catfish year-round," Collett says. "These deeper pools hold tons of catfish, lots of small and medium-sized cats, and the biggest cats in the river stay in these holes just about all of the time, I think."

Collett's favorite Tennessee River stretch is as familiar to him as his own backyard, but he still uses a depthfinder to locate new holes and position his boat properly when fishing over the top of these deep pools. "Any deep hole will hold an awful lot of catfish," he says, "but the best ones are very deep (in relation to the average depth of the river) and full of rocky cover." Collett says that his most productive, grade "A" river holes are usually 30 to 50 feet deep, and sometimes as deep as 70 feet. (Remember, however, that in a smaller river, good holes will be much shallower.)

This astute river rat understands the catfish's affinity for rock and capitalizes on it whenever possible. "Cats just like rock, especially big rocks," he says. "My very best holes tend to be littered with large rock or lined on at least one side with rocky shelves."

Through the years, Collett has put together a fishing system, utilizing the current flow. In essence, he simply drifts with the current while bouncing his baited rig off the bottom, directly under the boat. His terminal tackle rig consists of a 2-ounce sinker tied to the end of his 30-pound monofilament with a wickedly sharp 1/0 or 2/0 hook tied directly to the line about 12 inches above the sinker. Like most big river anglers of the Southeast, where shad is the predominant forage of virtually all predatory fish species, Collett baits his hooks with either live or whole dead shad, cut shad or shad guts.

Buckets of shad, like this one, are the trademark of serious catfishermen like Tim Collett. Shad are extremely effective as live bait and cut bait.

Collett says that heavy line used with sturdy baitcasting tackle is needed to successfully pull big cats out of these rough and rocky pools. Although many anglers would consider a 1/0 or 2/0 hook too small for monster cats, Collett deems it necessary to achieve a good hookset in this deep water. "Because monofilament stretches, it is very difficult to drive a thick hook into a catfish's tough mouth," he says. "When you're working 50 or 60 feet—or even more—beneath the boat, setting a hook can be a real problem. A smaller hook that is honed needle-sharp will penetrate much better than a larger one. And, I believe a top-quality 2/0 hook is strong enough to hold a giant cat. That is, if you play him correctly."

Before fishing one of his deep-river pools, Collett first "maps" it with his depthfinder, determining the hole's length, width, depth and general shape. He then positions his boat just upstream from the pool's forward slope and over to one side or the other. Next, he simply lowers his baited rig to the bottom directly under the boat and begins a downstream drift. "You've got to keep your bait right under the boat," he says. "If you drag it behind the boat, you'll hang up all the time."

While fishing the hole, Collett bounces the bait and heavy sinker rig off the bottom as he drifts downstream. He raises the rodtip a foot or two, then lowers it back down. As the hole deepens, he lets out more line but tries keeping the rig directly under the boat. The heavy, 2-ounce sinker helps to keep the rig perpendicular to the boat despite the current's pressure and the boat's downstream movement. Depending on the hole, some drifts may be as short as 100 yards or so. Others, particularly those along a river channel's outside bend or along a rocky, bluffy channel bank, may require a drift of a mile or so to cover the entire hole.

After making the first drift along one side of the hole, Collett motors back upstream and drifts down new territory. "I try to cover the hole completely," he says. "That's why I like to map it with the depthfinder before I start fishing. It may take 10 or 12 drifts and a whole morning to cover the entire hole just one time, but it's worth the effort. If you are catching cats from just one area, you can simply focus your attention there."

While smaller cats often peck at a bait chunk, Collett has found that decent fish, those over 10 pounds, will often smack a bait with the force of Babe Ruth's magic bat. "When a good catfish hits," he says, "you've got to set the hook very hard and try to get the fish moving upward as quickly as possible. If you don't get him off the bottom in just a few seconds, he will either cut your line on a rock or bury up under a ledge so you can't get him out."

Deep river holes are famous for producing catfish throughout the year. Apparently, however, some seasons are better than others. "I catch more cats from deep river pools during the hottest months of the year than I do at any other time," Collett says, "and I also catch more fish during the daylight hours than I do at night." That may surprise some anglers, but Collett theorizes that smaller fish leave the holes at night, probing shallower structure where forage is more prevalent. "I don't reckon the big cats leave their favorite holes though," he says, "because I catch them at all hours of the day or night."

Complete Angler's Library

Probing The River Bend

When Bob Holmes goes out catting, he often visits river bends. Holmes is a full-time outdoorsman and catfishing guide from Trenton, Tennessee, who retired from the "rat race" after suffering a heart attack some years ago. Daily fishing trips have taught him the ways of the cats. He has discovered several tactics that practically guarantee him and his clients tasty catfish on every fishing trip.

"One of my all-time favorite catfish structures is a dogleg in the river channel," Holmes says. "I concentrate on the outside edge of the channel bend where the current flows directly into the channel's side, rather than running along side it. If you think about it, you'll see that the current washes into this section of the channel. That means that it will also wash food into the area, and I believe the catfish congregate here for that reason." Also, cats like the river bend's outside edges because the water is usually much deeper than it is along the inside bend. Cats like depth.

We know that catfish move into the shallows to spawn in the early summer weeks. Shortly thereafter, Holmes says that they will begin showing up in these river bends. "I'll usually find them first holding at a depth of about 15 feet," he says, "but then they will rapidly move deeper as the summer progresses. By the time August rolls around, the catfish are usually holding in 35 to 40 feet of water." One of the obvious keys to Holmes' tactic is ascertaining the catfish's feeding depth, a determination typically made when locating fish on a depthfinder, then making experimental drifts at various depths. "When I am scouting," Holmes says, "schools of cats will usually show up on my LCR as a big black mass. I like to see shad on the depthfinder, especially when they are just 5 to 10 feet above the cats because that puts the fish in a feeding mood."

Like many of America's catfish fanatics, Holmes fishes to fill his frying pan. "I love to eat catfish," he says, "and I simply enjoy catching a lot of fish. For these reasons, I fish primarily for 2- to 5-pound cats." To make the hook-n-chase sequence a little more entertaining, Holmes opts for medium-weight bass tackle and 15-pound line. "Obviously, if I were fishing primarily for big cats, I'd use beefier tackle," he says. "We always hook into a good fish or two, and though this gear is awful light for a big catfish, we are able to land a great many of them."

Anatomy Of A River Bend

The outer edge of a river bend is typically much deeper than the inner edge. And, that deep-water hole is a favorite catfish haunt.

Complete Angler's Library

Holmes' terminal tackle rig is similar to Tim Collett's, except down-sized slightly. A ¾- to 1-ounce bell sinker ties to the line's terminal end. Next, a 6-inch surgeon's loop is tied in the line a few inches above the sinker, and a 1/0 or 2/0 hook slips onto the hanging line loop.

A big, juicy catalpa worm is his bait choice. However, because they are available for just a few weeks each summer, Holmes uses nightcrawlers more often. Fillets from the sides of river herring, which he catches by casting diminutive leadhead jigs below a dam, are another favorite; so are shad guts which are available in bait shops along the Tennessee River. "No matter what bait I use, I always spray it with an angling scent," he says. "I apply it whenever I put on a fresh bait, and then every time I take my bait out of the water. I believe cats feed predominantly by smell, so I think the addition of a scent is extremely important."

Finally, Holmes augments his rig with the addition of a small piece of plastic worm slipped onto the hook, covering the hook's eye. This is done for two reasons: First of all, it makes his offering a bit more buoyant. Secondly, it adds a little color to the bait, and Holmes believes that can be important at times. "More so than anything else, I think it attracts the cats to my bait," he says. "Kind of gets their attention. My favorite color is red, although I also have considerable success with chartreuse, blue and black."

Once rigged up and ready to fish, Holmes runs upstream and positions his boat over the river channel's outside edge and at a spot that has the desired depth. After dropping his bait to the bottom, he begins a downstream drift. "I try to maintain one specific depth on every drift," he says, "and I use the trolling motor to keep the boat positioned properly. The current will try to push you into the shallower edges of the bend, so you've got to bump the trolling motor on occasion to keep the boat in position. Keeping the nose of your boat pointed into the current will help you maintain proper boat position."

Like Collett, Holmes prefers keeping his bait directly under the boat at all times to avoid hang-ups. "I simply raise the bait a foot or two and then lower it back down as I drift down the dogleg's contour," he says. "Really, the technique is much like a bass angler jigging a spoon under the boat, or vertical jigging for sauger. Depending on the specific structure that I am fishing, my drifts may be as short as 100 yards or as long as half a mile.

Drifting in a river channel can result in catching some nice cats as this angler is doing here. Experts advise keeping the bait right under the boat so that it doesn't get snagged. It's a jigging technique that is similar to those used for bass and sauger.

"I prefer using this technique in rivers because I believe the current concentrates the fish. This same technique will work in reservoirs; the only difference is that you have to use your trolling motor to ease the boat along the side of the river channel."

Artificial Lures For Aggressive Cats

Most catfish anglers rely on natural baits of some sort, but Glenn Peacock uses an assortment of artificial lures when hunting river cats. Peacock, a veteran guide from Silver Spring, Maryland, fishes primarily on the Potomac River, which has always been one of the finest channel catfish rivers in the country. Flourishing aquatic vegetation recently has helped cleanse the river of silt and pollutants. These weedbeds filter silt and sediment from the waters, provide a sanctuary for the fry of all species and add oxygen to

Anchoring above a school of cats and jigging directly beneath the boat is often an effective way of catching cats. If you're on top of a bunch, stay with them.

Moving in close to bridge pilings and jigging directly below your boat can produce some nice strings of good-sized catfish who like to hug the rocks and vertical cement slabs.

the water. Fish populations in the river, including that of channel cats, have literally exploded in the past decade or so. Competition is keen among cats; they are feisty and aggressive.

Peacock capitalizes on the channel cats' aggression, much to the enjoyment of his clients, by offering them artificial lures. "It's a nice change from using smelly or bloody baits all of the time," Peacock says, "and it's very effective throughout the summer months—the hotter the better—for aggressive cats." One of his favorite techniques involves jigging a lipless, rattling crankbait like a Rat-L-Trap around the deeper bridge pilings in the actual river channel.

"We'll pull the boat in close to a piling, drop the bait down to a depth of about 10 feet, and then jig it for a few minutes. If we don't get a strike, we lower it another 10 feet and continue jigging," he says. His favorite pilings sit in 30 to 40 feet of water. While most fish hit near the bottom, enough cats strike in the shallower depths to make working them worthwhile. Peacock also trolls crankbaits to catch his river cats. "We normally rig one rod with a Rat-L-Trap and another with a deep-diving crankbait," he says. "That lets us cover two different depths. The Rat-L-Trap will run 2, maybe 3 feet deep, and the deep-diving crankbait will run about 10. We put those poles in rod holders on the back of the boat, then troll over main river structure such as humps, rock piles, flats with some sort of secondary channel running through them, or any other depth break that approaches to within 5 to 8 feet of the surface. I have found that sharp breaks from shallow water to deep—structure that are almost vertical in nature—tend to be most productive for me."

Anchors Away

Even though most catfish experts prefer drifting their baits when fishing larger rivers, some prefer the ease and relaxation of fishing from a stationary boat. Drifting can be tough, even hazardous at night. Anchoring your boat is a valid alternative. Although you cannot cover as much water, you can cover a hole quite thoroughly and give the cats plenty of time to respond to your offering.

The key here is to anchor over a potentially productive area, primarily on the forward (or upstream) segments of pools and river bends. The confluence of a tributary and the main river is another potential hotspot, but be sure to study the area thoroughly with your depthfinder so you can select a position that is near the actual channels.

Wherever you decide to fish, do not waste your time if the cats are not cooperating. Pull up anchor and move. Scout a bit. Try another spot. Sooner or later, you will find cooperative fish.

14

Fishing Ponds And Pay Lakes

Farm ponds—small pools providing water for cattle and livestock—have been popular catfish holes for more than a century. Pay lakes, or ponds where you simply pay to catch and keep catfish, are one of the country's top angling attractions. Well-managed ponds produce hoards of lunker cats and provide angling enjoyment and relaxation unparalleled in the field. And, as any veteran pond-angler can attest, small waters do not necessarily mean small cats.

Types Of Ponds

Most American ponds consist of three basic types of small water bodies; two are formed from some sort of dam. In essence, this means an angler can give the pond a quick once-over with a depthfinder and learn a great deal about catfish location in that specific water body.

The typical farm pond is a round or rectangular basin, either naturally generated or carved out of the ground with earth-moving equipment. Generally, they are the smallest bodies of fishable still water. In most instances, these ponds are fed from surrounding water runoff rather than from a creek or spring. These bowl-shaped ponds are deepest in the middle, with featureless, gradually sloping sides lacking any distinct depth breaks or "terra firma" structure.

Because most of these ponds lack structure, they have nothing (other than the deep central hole) to hold catfish. In rectangular

A nice-sized blue catfish such as this one can be your reward for checking out the small, farm ponds that many anglers overlook. The secret is to locate whatever current there may be within the pond.

ponds, however, the corners will hold catfish just as they would bass and bluegill. Adding man-made structure can easily improve farm ponds. Brush piles sunk midway between the shoreline and the pond's deepest point will hold cats throughout the year. Other types of added structure such as small, concrete culverts and fish attractors made from non-polluting materials will work, as well. Trees felled along the shoreline that drop into the pond also will attract cats.

Gutter dams, constructed across low-lying land, may impound a tiny creek, natural spring or surface runoff. Typically, a back-hoe or some type of mechanized shovel scoops up dirt, then piles it into a long dam stretching across a low expanse. This results in a relatively deep "gutter" running just in front of the dam's entire length.

In gutter-dam ponds, water depth usually increases as you move toward the dam. The deepest waters can be found along the dam's base. Fishing from the dam allows anglers to probe that deep hole and make long casts to the shallower areas where actively feeding cats often patrol.

Dams impounding a creek or spring, or dammed-creek ponds, are smaller than gutter-type dams, although the impoundment may be any size. Ten- to 50-acre ponds are common when creeks are dammed, although small lakes of a few hundred acres are possible. These dams usually span a relatively narrow expanse between two hills and may be quite high (depending upon the pond's depth). Dammed creeks normally have an overflow outlet regulating the water's height because of the influx of freshwater. In other words, dammed creeks always have freshwater running into them. To prevent overflowing the dam, these ponds have a stand-pipe or spillway that maintains a stable water depth and directs all excess water outside the pond.

Because dammed creeks and springs generally have a constant water supply running into them, and thus a slight current, they often do not stratify during the summer months. This is especially true in smaller ponds fed from sizable creeks. Ultimately, this means you can search and scour the pond's deeper portions and expect to catch cats throughout the summer.

Dammed-creek ponds have channels coursing across their bottoms, structure that catfish often prefer above all others. Depending upon the impounded creek's size, the pond may also

One of the first places to head for in fishing a small pond is the inflow/outflow point. Currents will be stronger in this part of the pond, and cats like currents.

cover a few secondary channels from old feeder streams and runoff ditches. Mapping these channel structures and focusing your attentions on them will lead you to catfish. That is a fact!

Catfish Location In Ponds

As a general rule, catfish will congregate in the deepest holes in any pond. (Note, however, that deep water often becomes uninhabitable to catfish when summer stratification occurs.) Thus, a farm pond's central hole, a gutter dam's front ditch and a dammed-creek pond's old creek channel offer superb catfishing opportunities. These deep holes also serve as the cats' wintering areas, so you can find catfish stacked up like cordwood during the colder months.

In small ponds, actively feeding cats can be found roaming the

Most small ponds have limited structure. Boat docks and piers provide cover and structure to the cats' liking. Docks are good spots, especially if people clean their fish there.

banks, searching for an easy meal. Look for points, pockets, weed-lines and even shady areas around the bank. Although floating lights are not normally used when catfishing, pond-bound cats often learn that dock lights attract baitfish and bluegills.

Any type of inflowing water attracts cats to an area. A flow of freshwater ignites feeding activity in catfish, especially when the influx is muddied and rich in terrestrial matter (often occurring during periods of heavy rainfall). Pond catfishing reaches its peak when muddied runoff races into the pond. Even if the water looks thick enough to stir, cats will probably be feeding there. Also, a pond's outflow area generally has a current. Cats position themselves in that current, no matter how slight.

Catfish particularly like rocks. Any rocky substrate, chunky riprap or bluff-type, rocky wall will be a gathering place for cats.

Catfish Baits For Catfish Ponds

A pond's available forage markedly differs from a larger impoundment or river's forage. Typically, the various species of bream and minnows comprise the largest portion of a pond cat's diet. Thus, live bluegill and minnows (or cut bait made from them) are often the best choice.

At one pond, frequented by the author, blue cats up to 50 pounds or more generally will shun nearly every bait. A giant, tail-hooked bluegill placed 3 to 4 feet under a large bobber will, however, pull those big cats off the bottom to investigate. And, when one decides to make a meal of that big bream, a furious, spellbinding, breathtaking topwater commotion ensues as the giant cat chases the bluegill around the surface. That strategy has put cats—mostly blues—as large as 43 pounds into the author's boat. Small waters do not necessarily mean small cats!

Other natural baits, like nightcrawlers, catalpa worms and crayfish, work well. Additionally, baits such as congealed blood, commercially prepared stinkbaits and chicken livers work best in a pond where competition among cats is keen. For this reason, pond cats feed aggressively and will pounce on unusual and unfamiliar bait far more readily than the lake-bound cats that habitually feed on shad.

Tom Mann, the legendary lure designer and tournament fisherman from Eufaula, Alabama, fishes for farm-pond cats with traditional bass lures. "Catfish in ponds have lots of competition," he says, "so they'll often fight to get to a bait. My favorite lures are rattling, lipless crankbaits. Sometimes, the cats will hit these baits when you retrieve them at high speeds near the surface, but I usually catch a lot more when I use a fairly slow retrieve that lets the bait bump along the bottom. And, talk about hitting a bait! A 5-pound cat will thump a lure harder than any bass that you have ever felt." Mann's strategy allows you to cover a lot of water quickly. Catfish really hit artificial lures!

Coping With Stratification

In the warmest summer months, many—perhaps even most—small lakes and ponds separate into three, distinct water layers. The warmest water layer is on the top and supports all the pond's living creatures. The lower stratum is cold and virtually devoid of oxygen, thus incapable of sustaining life. The thermocline, a narrow water band, separates these two layers.

Because ponds have little inflowing freshwater—thus, little or no current—they are more prone to thermal stratification than dammed rivers. Also, ponds are often set into a low-lying expanse of land, or sheltered in a small valley, and, therefore, not buffeted by the winds like a large expansive lake. (Wind creates waves that impart some type of current to a lake. In the case of a shallow lake, strong winds may create strong currents, keeping the lake from stratifying.)

In a stratified pond, catfish cannot live in the water's lower layer. Anglers casting baits on the bottom in the deepest water holes often fail to get even a nudge. (There are no cats there to begin with!)

How, then, do you catch these late-summer cats from a stratified pond? Suspend your baits under a bobber.

Catfish in a stratified pond often suspend on top of the thermocline. This is located at the lake's mid-depth point (but is sometimes found much shallower). Actually, catfish may lie on the thermocline just as if it were the pond's true bottom.

Most pond anglers suspend their bait first at approximately the pond's mid-depth. If there's no activity, they raise the bait 12 to 18 inches. This step is repeated until the angler finds the catfish's feeding and/or holding depth.

Aside from stream fishing, bobbers are most beneficial to catfish anglers when fishing a stratified pond. The familiar round, red and white, plastic or cork, clip-on type bobbers are fine for fishing close to shore. Anglers wishing to cover larger water expanses, however, will get better results from using 8- to 12-inch, cylindrical bobbers that look something like a totem pole. They not only provide sufficient weight for making long casts well out into the pond, but also offer enough height for adequate visibility at those increased distances. Even though these bobbers traditionally are made of balsa wood, plastic versions are more durable and can be rigged in many different ways. Some, in fact, are even illuminated, making them an angler's best choice for nightfishing. Anglers can use a different colored lightstick on each line, making line differentiation at night easier.

Pay-Lake Strategies

Pay lakes are one of the most popular fishing holes for catfish anglers across America. For a fee, some ponds let you keep all the cats you catch. Others impose a limit on the number of fish that may be kept. Still, other pay lakes charge you for each catfish caught; most often, the fish must be kept—catch-and-release is not allowed! Given the fact that fresh catfish fillets now sell for exorbitant prices in grocery stores, pay-lake fees are very reasonable (if you can catch any cats!).

Because pay lakes base their survival on anglers catching—and keeping—catfish from them, all are stocked periodically with fresh catfish, usually on a weekly basis. Most often, pay-lake fishing is excellent the evening after the lake is stocked with fish. Catfish easily cope with environmental changes and often feed ravenously after several days of foodless captivity. Thus, knowing a specific pay pond's stocking schedule leads to catfishing success.

By talking to the pond's owner or nearby neighbors, an angler can learn about the pond's underwater structure and identify deep holes, channels, or hidden inflow and outflow points.

If you plan on spending a long day or night at the pay lake, it may help to chum your fishing area. Toss out some minced fish or meat. Tie a small burlap or cheesecloth sack to a rope. Put in some dog and cat food, congealed blood or various fish and animal parts, along with a rock, and toss it into the pond. (Be sure to take the sack with you when you leave.)

Most anglers venturing to a pay-lake bait their hooks with worms, chicken livers or prepared baits. It may, then, behoove you to try something different. Big, live chub minnows or hand-sized bluegill might attract a big cat's attention, while cut bait or crayfish (whole, or just the peeled tail sections) may attract cats of any size.

Catfishing's
Special
Situations

15

Flat-Water Cats

ater, water everywhere! Looking at a typical, large impoundment overwhelms many anglers. Locating a catfish in all that space must surely be more difficult than finding a contented country boy in the confines of New York city.

Luckily, that is not the case. While America's largest impoundments may be imposing sights, catfish relate to structure in predictable ways. Learning to identify and locate the structure is vital to becoming a proficient, flat-water catfisherman.

Through The Seasons

Although lake-bound catfish respond to seasonal changes, their migrations are not as pronounced nor as directed as that of their cousins living in rivers and streams. Although no one seems to know exactly why this is true, many theorize that reservoir catfish simply have a lot of deep water available to them at any time. After all, if you own a nice, spacious house and your roof does not leak, you have no reason to move.

In every impoundment in the country, catfish move into the shallows during late spring. This migration is a spawning phenomenon, resulting in a few weeks of difficult fishing for many anglers. The cats abandon their deep-water haunts, leaving some fishermen wondering, "Where did they go?" Ken Nelms refers to this period as the "May slump," although it can occur in June or July. Obviously, catfish did not disappear; you just have to know where

Finding cats in lakes can be a real challenge. In late spring, catfish move into the shallows for spawning. Checking these traditional spawning areas can be profitable.

to find them. Focusing your attention on traditional spawning habitats will help you take catfish. Although this slump generally lasts about six weeks or so, anglers can usually find a few fish in the deeper regions. This is because all cats do not spawn at one time.

Once catfish complete spawning, they usually head to deeper water. In many reservoirs, the most productive catfish areas are around old river channels. From the headwaters to the dam, these channels offer the deepest water in the lake. Many believe that catfish use river channels as highways, connecting their favorite structure. Secondary channels, such as creek arms and tributary channels, serve as secondary routes providing catfish with lanes to the shallows and shorelines. In some deep, expansive impoundments, overall depth throughout the major portions of the lake provides cats with comfort and security. The old channels, then, are less vital to the catfish.

These whiskered denizens of the deep hold in deep water as long as they can. If the lake stratifies, and a thermocline develops, it forces the catfish to move to shallower structure at the thermocline level, or slightly above it. Once the lakes turn over and the dissolved-oxygen levels throughout the depths are satisfactory for the cats, they will again move to deeper water.

Typically, catfish hang around the same deep structure in the winter as they did in summer. Often, there is no transition period between the summer and winter. However, at other times and in other impoundments, cats may move onto shallower structure in the fall, taking advantage of cooling water temperatures and abundant forage.

Super Structure
In most American impoundments, NAFC Members will find that structure fishing is the key to catfish success. Bass anglers take great pride in their structure fishing techniques, a bassing tactic which, by sportfishing standards, is still a smooth-cheeked youngster. But, catfish anglers have been fishing offshore structure for more than a century, and they often do it far better than their counterparts in shiny boats. Their technique was not heralded by fanfare and magazine articles, but welcomed simply as a better way to catch more fish.

Catfish utilize offshore structure as both a sanctuary and a feeding ground. For this reason, the most productive structure has

When cats head out into deeper water, your knowledge of the lake's topography will help you find them. Look for deep holes, old river channels and breaks.

some sort of shallower feeding or ambush area close to a deeper sanctuary. Structure located near a channel is most productive.

Vertical drops such as channel breaks, standing walls in old house foundations, submerged bridge pilings and inundated pond dams are particularly productive catfish-holding structure. Often, you will find the largest cats holding along the bottom of vertical structure, while smaller fish scout the bottom's shallower reaches.

One of the finest cat-holding structures on an impoundment is an underwater hump or submerged island. A topographical map identifies humps as a series of concentric rings on contour lines. If the depth numbers grow progressively smaller when moving toward the center of the circles, you have discovered a hump. (If the depths grow larger, you have found a depression, and it, too, may be worth investigating.)

Humps positioned close to a channel will be more productive than humps located on a shallow, flat, expansive bottom, lacking a deep-water sanctuary. However, a large hump sitting on a deep flat may hold a lot of cats, because it offers the only nearby structure, with catfish concentrating in that area.

In a stratified lake, a hump which is situated so its shallowest point intersects, or climbs, slightly above the thermocline will be one of the most productive—if not *the* most productive—structure you can fish. On smaller humps, the shallowest reaches hold the most actively feeding catfish. On larger humps, however, scout the structure with your depthfinder to find key holding areas. Look for stumps, brush piles, rock piles, depth breaks or any specific structure that may hold catfish. In this instance, you are actually searching for a smaller, specific structure on top of another, larger structure.

Channels often meet all the catfish's needs and become prime catfishing honeyholes, especially when the channel is well defined (i.e. when the channel's sides, or walls, are steep, near-vertical structure) and courses through a relatively shallow impoundment. To find the largest cat concentrations, scout the channel with a depthfinder to locate deeper holes, rock piles or major depth breaks. The channel bend's outside edge is a traditional hotspot. And, when the channel runs against a vertical, rocky bluff, stop and fish for a few minutes, and keep a tight grip on your rod!

Currents And Flat-Water Cats

Although many impoundments appear to be giant pools of still, lifeless water, most have some degree of current from time to time. In many cases, a current, or a lack thereof, becomes a critical element in the war against the whiskerfaces.

Flood-control lakes receive runoff during periods of heavy rain. That water influx is quickly offset by releasing the same water amount through the dam. In this fashion, the lake remains a stable pool. This inflow and outflow of water, however, imparts a current throughout the lake, all the way from the headwaters to the dam. In other impoundments, heavy rainfall creates an appreciable flow within the lake. Not throughout the lower impoundment, perhaps, but certainly in the headwaters and in any tributary or feeder stream.

This 20-pound blue catfish was pulled from an old river channel in a large impoundment. Some experts believe catfish use the channels as highways to get to various feeding grounds.

River-run lakes are the narrow impoundments coursing through hilly terrain which result from erecting a dam across a river. In most situations, the river channel consists of much of the lake bottom, with very little inundated floodplain. The lake, then, is simply the river's upward extension. Because the lake is narrow, a continuous current (and very often a strong one) flows through it. At the same time, fresh water runs into the lake, being matched by a similar amount which is released through the dam.

In most instances, creation of lake current, or the increased flow of an existing current increases catfish activity and foraging. Increased runoff carries a plenitude of food into the water. Main lake currents push baitfish around and generally stir things up.

Power-generating impoundments, or those whose primary function is hydroelectric-power generation, have intermittent current periods. When the generating tubes in the dam open, allowing water to flow through to spin the turbines, a current develops throughout the lake. Initially, the current begins in the impoundment's lower reaches, and it may take a few minutes (or up to an hour or more) before the waters in the lake's upper part begin moving.

Many anglers believe fishing becomes more productive when power is generated in this type of impoundment. At this time, catfish, as well as other fish species, abound. Feeding activity for the fish is intricately linked to current flow, with the most active feeding period occurring in the first hour of water movement. It does not matter whether the turbines start at 1 p.m. or 1 a.m.; peak catfish activity periods and catfishing productivity follow the generating schedules, rather than the time of day or night.

Hydroelectric power usually is generated on a schedule, according to the electrical needs of consumers. Agencies operating these generation stations most often determine their generating schedules approximately 24 hours prior to the event. Those schedules are available to the public. You can call, or often they are published in newspapers or posted in marinas. Although the schedules are subject to change, the angler would be wise to plan the next day's fishing around these generating periods.

Flat-Water Giants

Imagine fishing in Kentucky Lake, widely regarded as one of the country's finest catfish fisheries, with a spinning rod and 12-pound line. The rhythmic thump-thump-thump of the 1-ounce sinker striking bottom is suddenly interrupted by a bone-jarring yank, followed immediately by the squeal of your spinning reel as line peels from the reluctant spool. Your sweaty palms and palpitating heart threaten to lose this battle for you, but you compose yourself and begin chasing after the battling behemoth with the help of your trolling motor's 24-volt system. Some 15 agonizing minutes later, the monstrous catfish surfaces and, as blues so often do, begins rolling up in your whisper-thin line. Before the old blue can part your line, you ease the boat to him and watch with a pounding chest as your trusted buddy slips a net over the giant's head. Your buddy's yell for help snaps you out of a daze and, working together, you drag some 77 pounds of angry, thrashing catfish flesh into the boat.

Although this may sound like a dream come true, a once-in-a-lifetime occurrence, Darrell Van Vactor routinely enjoys days such as this one. A veteran fishing guide with many years of experience, Van Vactor has discovered a wonderfully productive, big-cat technique that puts scores of giant cats into his boat year after year.

"Big catfish, I think, are ambush feeders for the most part," Van Vactor says. "Their enormous size virtually prohibits them from chasing a much more agile baitfish, so they find themselves a good spot to lie and wait for the baitfish to come to them."

Van Vactor says many of the lake's largest cats position themselves in predictable locations along the intersection of a creek channel or ditch and the main river channel from about mid-August to mid-October. "I think that the big cats actually dig themselves a depression in the down-current side of that intersection where a creek channel meets the old river channel; then, they will remain right there for two to three months," he says. "The current actually sweeps almost directly into this location, and I believe the cats utilize the current as an aid in their foraging. They let the current bring the food to them."

Fishing tends to be the most productive when there is some current in the lake. Van Vactor's big-cat system is a specialized affair. In his Kentucky Lake stomping grounds, he discovered that large fish typically hold in 30 to 38 feet of water. "I'll catch some fish deeper than that," he says, "and, a lot of cats shallower than 30 feet, but my biggest fish always come between 30 and 38 feet deep."

Believe it or not, Van Vactor uses nothing but medium-action spinning gear and 12-pound line. "We fish for fun," he says, "and a 50-pound catfish will give you all of the fun that you can handle on 12-pound line!" His rig is simple, consisting of a 1-ounce egg sinker toothpicked onto the line about 12 inches above a 4/0 stainless hook honed razor sharp. If you would prefer a little insurance, heavier tackle will work, too. If you want to try Van Vactor's light tackle approach, he recommends using a 6½- or 7-foot, medium-action spinning rod, a high-capacity spinning reel with a top-quality drag, and a premium monofilament line.

"Big catfish didn't get big by being dumb," Van Vactor says. "And, I strongly believe that fresh, live bait is the key to catching bigger catfish. They have grown accustomed to eating live baitfish, and prefer eating live baitfish, so you should offer them what they want." For bait, he prefers 4- to 5-inch herring, which he catches using minuscule grubs and jigs in the roiling waters of the Kentucky Dam tailrace. They are difficult to keep alive, but Van Vactor can keep 12 or so in an aerated livewell. He warns anglers about overcrowding these fragile baitfish. When rigging the herring, he hooks them just behind the dorsal fin, and quickly lowers them to the bottom.

Like most experienced catfish anglers, Van Vactor prefers to remain on the move, easing over a potentially productive structure with the help of the wind, current or a trolling motor. Using a heavy, 1-ounce lead chunk, he probes the bottom, raising his rig and lowering it back to the bottom while trying to keep his bait directly underneath the boat.

How successful is Van Vactor's intersecting channel technique? Recently, he and his smiling clients put blue cats weighing 77, 68, 54 and 46 pounds into his boat. Another 12 blues between 35 and 42 pounds were taken along with hundreds of 3- to 15-pounders. "You hear about catfish being thought of as river fish," he says, "but I honestly believe that there are more big catfish in our large impoundments than there are in most of our rivers." With that kind of success, it is tough to argue with this expert!

Cats Love Caves

Catfish like to hold in deep, dark cubbyholes. Some theorize that cats like holes and caves because they give their soft skin some protection, provide security and offer superb ambush points. Whatever the case may be, the fact remains that cats love holes.

One overlooked hotspot in reservoirs is a culvert. Nearly every man-made impoundment in the country has a series of flooded roads which were covered when the lake water rose. Culverts and bridges may be found at almost every place where these old roads happened to cross a ditch, creek or the old river itself. In some instances, especially where bridges or culverts were in the lake's shallows posing a potential hazard for boating traffic, these objects were destroyed. But, those in deeper water, the ones most likely to hold catfish, were often left intact.

To find these hidden hotspots, look carefully at a topographic map of the impoundment's underwater structure. Most show the location of old roads that existed before the lake's impoundment.

One of the benefits of catfishing is the sights that you might not experience if you weren't out on a lake looking for cats.

Find those points where the old roads crossed a ditch, valley, creek or the old river. Then, using a liquid crystal sonar unit or paper graph, scout these areas by boat. Culverts and bridges typically show up as a symmetrical combination of horizontal and vertical structure. Although the cave under the bridge or culvert will not be visible, you can safely assume that it does exist.

Anchor on top of the structure so baits can be lowered to the culvert's mouths. The tactic calls for stout tackle and heavy line, since you may be forced to tow a giant cat out of its rocky or concrete lair. Remember, hit him hard, hit him fast and try to get the fish moving toward you as quickly as possible.

Schooling In Winter

In the winter months, catfish congregate in relatively large schools, gravitating to deep-water sanctuaries. Until the lake's water temperature drops into the 30s, catfishing can be fast and furious when you locate a school. In those lakes where water temperatures remain above 40 degrees or so throughout January and February, superb catfishing may be found throughout the winter.

Bob Fincher has cultivated a cold-weather catfishing technique, extending his fishing season to 12 months. "Catfish begin moving toward deeper water in the early weeks of fall," Fincher says. "I believe that a change in the length of the day (the photoperiod), or perhaps a change in the length of the night, signals the catfish and lets them know that winter is on the way. Then, they begin moving to deep-water sanctuaries where they will stay until spring." Fincher begins finding cats in these deep areas in mid-September. He says if the lake stratifies during the summer, the fish will start easing into deep water as soon as the lake turns over.

His favorite cat-holding structure is located along the old river channel's deep walls, or structure within the river channel itself. "I look for the standing timber, stump fields, rock piles, large boulders and rocky ledges," he says. "... any type of structure that catfish traditionally favor. In most large impoundments, I like to fish 35 to 70 feet deep throughout the winter."

Fincher says many of the same deep-water areas that held cats throughout the summer months will also hold cats during the winter. "The lake may stratify, causing the cats to abandon these deep holes in late summer," he says. "But, a good catfish hole in any reservoir will hold a bunch of cats throughout the year with the exception of the spawning period in late spring and early summer, and then during the time frame when the lake is stratified. Other than those times, the holes should be loaded with cats."

After locating potential hotspots by keeping a learned eye on his depthfinder, Fincher positions his boat over the structure and lowers his baited rig to the bottom. His preferred offering, by the way, is his own mixture of congealed blood bait slipped onto his two-hook hanging loop rig. Next, he pulls the bait a few inches off the bottom so it hangs vertically in the water. After placing his rods in rod holders, or laying them in the boat with their ends extending over the water, he watches the rodtips. "Cats don't usually hit very hard when the water is cold," he says. "When a strike occurs, all you will see is the rodtip shaking a little, kind of like a crappie taking a minnow."

While catfishing in an impoundment seems akin to searching for a needle in a haystack, it is not the case. Concentrate on offshore structure. Look for sharply defined depth breaks and vertical walls. If you anchor, do not spend too much time in any one spot. If the cats are not cooperating, try another spot. Drift techniques—either drifting with the wind or current, or slow-trolling with your trolling motor—allow you to cover an enormous amount of water, and let you take the game to the cats. Impounded catfish are, in a sense, bottled up and at your mercy!

=====16=====

Tailrace Tactics

Centuries ago, American Indians built a "dam-trap" across smaller rivers to catch, among other things, catfish. But, it was not until the 1930s that the first giant hydroelectric dams were built. Catfishing soon became firmly entrenched beneath these concrete monstrosities. Today, fishing the tailraces—the swift-water, outflow areas below dams—is one of the finest catfishing techniques known to rod-and-reel anglers.

Why Tailraces Are Popular

In simple terms, catfish like tailraces because baitfish like tailraces. The swift waters below dams harbor tons of shad, providing quick, convenient meals for cats. Additionally, entire shad schools, along with various other fish, often are swept from the lake through the dam's hydroelectric turbines. Many of these baitfish are minced, chopped and ground in the process, while others are simply left dazed and defenseless. Either way, these baitfish and their parts become easy catfish pickings.

Many expert tailrace anglers believe cats lie in well-chosen places below the dams, rarely moving throughout the year. These fish rapidly grow because their food supply is practically limitless and they expend very little energy when foraging. In essence, tailraces offer cats an abundance of food; if the aquatic environment is suitable, they have no reason to leave. Thus, tailrace areas provide year-round homes for catfish.

Tailraces probably are the closest thing to catfish heaven. Tim Collett's son (in background) caught this nice, 15-pound blue within shouting distance of this Tennessee dam.

Tailrace Tactics

Tailrace catfishing tends to be good throughout the year; however, it is often superb, magnificent and almost "heavenly" in the pre- and post-spawn periods. Catfish migrate especially in late spring or early summer. When catfish leave their wintering holes in the spring, they begin an upstream journey, searching for food and good spawning areas. High-water and heavy-flow periods (typical of a wet spring) spur catfish migration. If a dam blocks their way, cats literally pile up below it in monstrous numbers.

Turbines Of Plenty

Hydroelectric, power-generating dams which use a constricted water flow to create electricity are scattered across the country. Perhaps, the most famous are the Tennessee Valley Authority (TVA) projects distributed along the Tennessee River system through Tennessee, Alabama, Kentucky, Georgia and North Carolina. Although these dams come in all sizes, from the concrete monstrosities spanning a mile or more to small dams bridging a mountain chasm, the power-generating area usually is confined to one small portion of the dam and is fitted with many power-generation turbines. The tailrace is the outflow from the turbine.

Tim Collett, an avid and accomplished catfish angler from Lenoir City, Tennessee, has mastered the art of tailrace fishing. "You can catch catfish from tailraces all year long," he says, "but the best time is usually during the two months of the spawn. There are more catfish below dams at that time, I think, than all of the rest of the year combined. And, anytime the water rises below a dam, as during a flood, or anytime that water flow through the dam is increased, catfishing just gets better." Collett also says that a wet, rainy spring that raises the water level usually results in superb catfishing below the dam.

Collett believes outflow points from power-generating turbines force the fish into predictable locations. "Currents are tremendously strong when the turbines are running," he says. "Fish don't really like to fight current, but all of them—baitfish and catfish, too—like to feed in it. Current brings the food to the fish, so they will position themselves just out of the strongest currents and wait for the food to be swept by them."

When water flowing through turbine chutes exits beneath the dam, it is directed against large, concrete blocks often referred to

Fishing in a spillway's outflow isn't for the faint-hearted, and is illegal in many areas. Many anglers find a seam and move their boats close to the structure, and then drag their baits on the bottom as they drift downstream. Then, they go back and repeat the process.

as alligator claws. Those blocks break up the tremendously strong water flow that could create unmanageable downstream currents, eroding much of the river bottom. When water strikes these alligator claws, it goes upward and produces the typical water "boil" familiar to all tailrace anglers. With two turbines operating side by side, a relatively vague "seam" in the downstream current develops along the line where the two currents meet. This seam of decreased current flow is a focal point for knowledgeable anglers.

"Both the catfish and the baitfish hold in that seam in the current," Collett says. "And, in my experience, it is the most productive spot in the entire tailrace."

Collett uses a drift system when fishing these turbine seams. After driving his boat to a turbine's boil base, he makes a short cast (approximately 20 feet) directly between the boils. With the outboard still in gear, Collett holds the boat in position while his baited rig drifts back to the boat. Once that happens, he moves the boat on top of the seam and cuts the engine, allowing the boat to drift downstream on the current seam. "The goal is to get the bait down near the bottom and under the boat before you cut the engine and start your drift," he says. "It is much easier and much more productive if you can keep your bait directly under the boat at all times, even though that is often hard to do in these strong currents. When tailraces are full of cats and you make a good drift, you will either hook a fish or lose your bait with every downstream float."

Although current seams typically stretch 20 to 40 yards downstream, Collett continues drifting as much as 300 yards downstream. "Most of the fish strike very near the turbines," he says, "but you catch enough fish on downstream to make the long drift worthwhile. Besides, it's more enjoyable that way. If you try to keep the boat in the seams all the time, you will work yourself to death; to me, that takes the fun out of fishing."

Collett's tackle rig is very basic. "Tailraces are notorious for stealing your hooks and sinkers," he says, "so you want to keep it simple; something you can retie very quickly." On the end of his 20-pound line, Collett ties a 2-ounce sinker, providing enough weight to pull the bait down through the currents to the bottom. A 3/0 hook is tied directly to the line about 12 inches above the sinker. Although he uses heavy-duty bass tackle (i.e., a flipping stick and a sturdy reel), many anglers use heavier gear. "I use 20-pound line because I can break it without too much trouble when I hang the rig on the bottom," he says. "I've used heavier line. But, when you hang up and the current is pulling you rapidly downstream, you are apt to lose your rod and reel or go overboard if you can't break that line."

Collett believes in using the natural bait most abundant to the catfish. In a tailrace, that most likely is shad. "I net shad with a dip net and toss them into a bucket for use as cut bait," he says. "I'll cut a 6- or 8-inch shad into three or four pieces, and my favorite chunks are the gut sections."

In some places, engineers stretch cables across the turbine outflow area a few feet above the surface, preventing anglers from driving their boats near the boiling currents. Although the current seams may be off limits, anglers still catch fish. One preferred

Drift fishing through the turbine boils and current seams can be one of the deadliest tactics for catching big cats known to American catfish anglers. It can pay big dividends.

tactic is tying the boat to the cable and fishing the bottom with heavy weights and tackle. You can also lower your baited hook weighted with a ½- to 1-ounce sinker into the water, and slowly feed out line from the reel, allowing the bait to ease downstream at a snail's pace. Anglers often tie their boats to steel rings set into the dam's concrete sidewalls and fish directly under the boat.

The catfishing productivity of a hydroelectric tailrace depends upon the turbine's operation. When turbines operate, catfish feed readily and in predictable locations. A turbine's operation, and the water flow through it, depends upon the area's electrical demands. Typically, electrical demand is highest during summer weekdays and lowest during weekend nights of late spring, summer and early autumn. Knowing the power-generating schedules helps when planning your fishing trips.

Fishing Below A Longwall Dam

As indicated in this diagram, catfish will settle in the hole on the face of the longwall, as well as moving to the top of the rocks that help form the hole.

A large gate lowered to block the water flow through the turbine chute turns off the hydroelectric, power-generating turbines. Thus, when turbines turn off, no water flows through them and no currents are created. Unless water is released from another gate in the dam, the tailrace becomes as still as a sheltered pond. Baitfish scatter. Catfish scatter. Fishing becomes tough. Time to call it a night.

Longwall Tactics

Dams spanning a wide chasm between hills or mountains usually have a long, concrete wall (called the "longwall") filling the large expanse. If a hydroelectric station is built into the dam, it will usually be at one end of the dam; and, most of the released water will flow through its turbines. By comparison, dams without turbine generation release water through a tunnel-like spillway often at one end of the dam.

The longwall normally has a series of floodgates on top that can be opened to increase water flow during a potential flood situation. To break up the overflow from the floodgates, large rocks and boulders are often piled into a wedge, or flat, just downstream from the longwall. They reduce the current's force just like the alligator claws do in a turbine discharge area. Ultimately, a deep ditch develops between the longwall and this current break—a canal that holds catfish.

That current break's shallow lip often serves as a hotspot for catfish anglers. While the deepest portion of the ditch or canal acts as a sanctuary, the shallower areas are a quick, convenient feeding ground. Cats will roam the entire rocky structure, but activity seems to center around that slope from shallow water to deep. And, don't overlook the deep-water sanctuary for success.

Because these areas are rather large and removed from the direct current flow, they cannot be fished very well by using a current drift. Instead, anchor over the top of the lip and cast a few bottom rigs around the boat. If you prefer remaining on the move, try drifting with the wind or easing around with the trolling motor while bouncing a bait off the bottom directly under the boat. These current breaks can be particularly rough on your terminal tackle. Bouncing your bait vertically under the boat can minimize snags, tackle loss and conserve fishing time.

Catfish often spawn in the rocky crevices of current breaks that are within 4 to 6 feet of the surface. While there is no hard, firm evidence supporting that fact, it does make sense. Besides, experts like Tim Collett believe this to be true. For whatever reason, catfish are found in these rocky areas during the spawning season, often pouncing on bait bounced off the bottom. If you think cats may be spawning there, try this: Slip a piece of cut bait onto a 1-ounce, leadhead jig and probe the bottom with it. The round, heavy jig rolls off the rocks and into the holes underneath. If a nesting cat is there, it will smash the bait. Hit it hard and fast. Try pulling the fish out of its subterranean lair as quickly as possible. Obviously, you should use heavy lines and stout tackle.

Scouring The Spillways

When water from the main lake is released into the tailrace

Working the spillways, as Tim Collett is doing here, can be a highly effective method of catching cats whose migration up the river has been blocked by the dam.

below through a tunnel-like spillway, the angler can assume that the amount of fresh water running into these lakes is usually quite small. The amount of water flowing through a spillway will fluctuate widely because it depends upon the lake level above it. During periods of heavy rains, or when the lake level is lowered, the spillway's water flow may be enormous. On the other hand, flow will be minimal or non-existent when the lake level is rising. When the lake is at normal level and rainfall is stable, the water flow through the spillway should remain moderate and stable.

As a general rule, high-water flow often attracts catfish into the tailrace. The increased water flow provides an abundance of food, and cats move upstream to take advantage of it. However, long periods of stable or decreased flows usually result in a drop in the catfish population directly below the spillway.

Finding Catfish In Spillways

The breaks at the end of the spillway create current boils that create holes at the base of the spillway. The boils also create current seams which catfishermen can use to their advantage.

Spillways have current breaks just like turbine discharges. These breaks often serve as the activity center for both catfish and angler. Cats seek shelter from the current behind these breaks while watching for an easy meal in the moving waters. Although current breaks in a spillway are not as evident as the breaks that cause enormous boils in a hydroelectric discharge flow, sharp-eyed anglers can locate them by watching the surface closely. When water flows into a break, it then travels upward, usually creating some sort of surface disturbance. Find these little boils and roils and you will find catfish.

Spillways can be fished in virtually any manner. Drifting is probably the most effective method, although many spillway-type tailraces are too small to permit passage of anything other than a small boat. In some cases, walkways and concrete platforms edge

Always remember that tailraces are extremely dangerous areas. Currents are strong and unpredictable. Even if you're fishing from the bank, keep safety in mind at all times.

the spillway on two or three sides, providing bank anglers easy access to the small tailrace.

Dams and locks spanning many of the country's smaller rivers form an effective barrier that catfish cannot cross. Therefore, cats congregate below them. In most cases, there won't be man-made current breaks beneath the outflow or overflow points of these dams, so locating potential catfish-holding structure is more difficult. Search for a channel with your depthfinder. Watch the surface for boils and disturbances—any evidence of structure lurking below. And, pay attention to current patterns.

Feast Or Famine?

Tailraces concentrate cats in the pre-spawn period and hold them until the spawn is complete. Fishing is fast and furious.

Catch 20 cats one day, and 40 more may move in overnight.

Many catfish then drift downstream after leaving their spawning nests, finally settling into deeper river holes for the summer. As summer progresses, more and more cats leave the tailrace. Sure, some will remain there all year, but not in the numbers that made fishing during the pre-spawn period so productive.

Tailraces are readily visible, easily accessible targets for many anglers. Thus, fishing pressure takes its toll on the catfish population. During the summer months, better catfishing usually can be found just downriver from the dam.

A word of caution: A dam's tailrace currents can be wickedly strong and always unpredictable. For your own safety, *wear* a personal flotation device.

=17=

Absentee Catfishing

Catfish have been a major food source for North American inhabitants for centuries. Because they were, at one time, vital to humans for survival, our angling predecessors developed many ways to take catfish with little effort. In fact, enough cats could be taken overnight (while anglers slept) to feed their families and tribes. This freed the daylight hours for other tasks. Two of these techniques, trotlining and limblining, can be attributed to the ancient North American Indians.

Centuries ago, the Indians used lines made of hemp, hair or sinew, and hooks fashioned from the toe bone of whitetailed deer. Today's anglers use synthetic lines and steel hooks, but the techniques themselves have changed very little. Even though very few now need to catch catfish to survive, trotlining and limblining are two tactics that provide quality entertainment night after night, as well as enough fish to support the largest, Sunday-afternoon fish-fries.

Trotline Tactics

Catfishing with virtually any angling method is both fun and productive, but trotlining is historically the most productive hook-and-line technique used to catch these whiskered denizens of the deep. Some consider this method boring. Others somehow believe they can catch more catfish with a rod and reel than with a multi-hooked trotline. But, for catching a lot of catfish, noth-

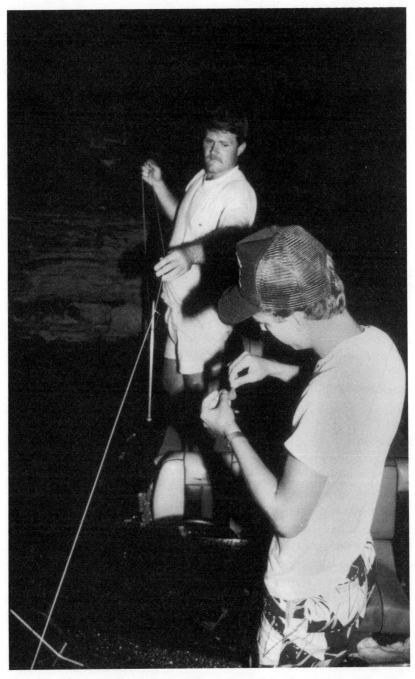

Having good light available is important when setting, baiting and running a trotline at night. Whether it's done during day or night, however, it's much easier to do with two people.

Absentee Catfishing

ing, absolutely nothing, can beat a well-placed trotline.

Trotline Construction

A trotline is a long, hook-filled line which stretches across a river or buoys in a lake or reservoir. The hooks are baited, and the trotline checked after a period of time. Most often, lines are set and baited just before sundown, then checked sometime the next morning.

The trotline's main line is much larger in diameter than the staging lines, making it easier to handle. When running (checking and baiting) a trotline, most anglers grasp the main line and pull themselves along it. Although some catfishermen use main line as thin as 250-pound test, a larger line (at least 600-pound test) works best because it is easier on the hands.

The main-line length varies with the river or area width to be covered, and the number of hooks used. Generally, trotlines will be 100 to 250 feet in length. Shorter droplines hang from the main line, and hooks are attached to these staging lines.

When catfish are hooked, they twist and turn trying to free themselves. If they can obtain some form of "hold" or something to twist against, they often twist off the line. Thus, precautions must be taken to avoid losing fish. To prevent catfish from twisting to freedom, the droplines should hang from swivels on the main line. Don't tie the swivels to the main line, however, because catfish could wrap the dropline around the main line. Instead, the swivels should be slipped onto the main line at 2- to 4-foot intervals, held in place with crimp-on metal brads available from commercial tackle outfitters, net supply companies and some hardware stores.

Droplines (or stagings), normally made of 100-pound-test line tied to swivels, vary in length between 12 and 24 inches; 18 inches is ideal. A "hanging loop" dropline is the best for attaching hooks and making exchanges quickly. To form an 18-inch dropper, use 36 inches of line. Pass the line's two loose ends together through the swivel's eye and tie a suitable knot, leaving an 18-inch hanging loop of line. To attach the hook, pass the loop through the hook's eye, then over the hook point. Now, pull the line back through the eye while snugging the loop against the hook shank's back. This will tighten the line. It takes just a second, and it is stronger than a knot. Also, it is wise to tie a simple figure-eight

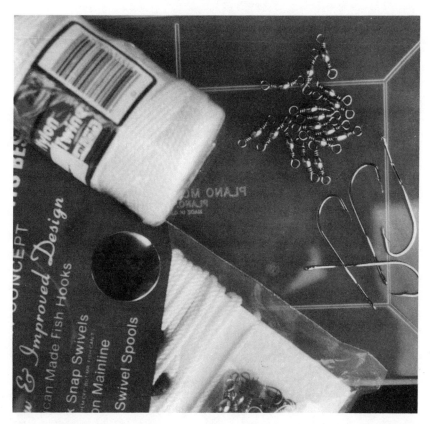

This is the basic package for trotlining. It includes a heavier cord for the main line, and lighter line for the drops, swivels and hooks.

knot in the hanging loop a few inches above the hook. The more secure, the better.

Hook size should depend upon the size of bait used. Generally, 2/0 to 5/0 forged, heavy-duty hooks are preferred. Because cats usually take a trotlined bait deep into their mouths and sometimes even swallow it, long-shanked hooks will be easier to remove. Trotlines are typically left in the water for an extended time period. Many catfish experts prefer stainless steel hooks. This is because they are much more rust- and corrosion-resistant than the carbon-steel ones.

When constructing a trotline, use synthetic fiber (nylon or polyester) lines. Natural fibers like cotton or hemp will rot in a relatively short time. Most tackle shops and department stores carry all the materials you need for a quality trotline.

Trotline storage is a problem for most anglers. Commercial spools are available, or you can wrap the trotline around a coffee can or, in this case, a block of Styrofoam.

Setting The Trotline

Your trotlining success will depend largely on your skill at placing the line among feeding cats. Because rivers and impoundments are full of catfish, and receive surprisingly little angling pressure, this is normally not difficult. Trotlines set virtually anywhere will produce a few cats, but trotlines set in a prime location will most often be full of fish when you run it the next morning. If you are not happy with the catch, move the line.

In a river or stream, trotlines are normally set across an expanse of moving water. In larger streams where this is not possible or feasible, simply tie one end to the bank and the other out in the river. Because deep water pools hold the largest numbers of cats, trotlines should be set over these pools. In areas directly below a tributary inlet, catfish feed along the bank. In this circumstance, set your trotline so it runs parallel to the bank immediately downstream from the feeder creek. Stream trotlines are normally set so the hooks dangle near the bottom.

In reservoirs, the trotline depth is crucial to success. In lakes which are not thermally stratified, success can usually be guaranteed if the trotline sets are near the bottom around rocky, offshore structure situated close to the inundated river channel. In stratified impoundments, position trotlines (usually with floating jugs) above the thermocline level. Trotlines in impoundments harboring large blue-cat populations should be buoyed so they are a few feet below the surface. This will often produce more blues than those lines that are weighted to the lake's bottom. Blue cats roam through the depths searching for food. Often, great schools of blues will range together, following enormous shad and herring schools that meander through these impoundments.

Look for channel breaks and sharp ledges, the main river channel, secondary channels, rock piles and humps and riprapped areas (bridges, dams and road facings) when setting a trotline. Basically, success can be guaranteed if you can find any structure offering a sudden drop, a hard rocky substrate and both shallow and deep water close to each other.

While deep-set trotlines will catch fish both day and night, the best success (in terms of numbers of fish) at night usually comes on a trotline set in shallow water. Most of a lake's forage is found in the shallows. Catfish, like all other gamefish that feed at night, move into the shallows to take advantage of the abundant forage found after sunset. Thus, points and flats should not be overlooked when setting your trotlines. Small cats are especially prone to foraging in the shallows. The largest cats, however, typically haunt a deep-water hole, seldom leaving it unless forced to do so.

When setting a trotline, be sure to attach one end of the line to a flexible object, or something that can provide some "give" to the line. Most often, trotliners attach one end of the line to a tree branch. The branch acts as a shock absorber for the line and keeps a giant cat from having anything solid to pull against so you don't lose the larger cats. If the line can give, the cat will wear itself out without pulling off of the hook, breaking a dropper line or straightening a hook.

To keep the line near the bottom, trotline weights should be

Trotlining is a popular way to catch catfish, as indicated by this angler who is surveying his catch. Because the main line is submerged, you won't know you've got a fish until you raise the dropline.

attached at intervals along the line. A traditional favorite is a 3- to 5-pound window weight, although bricks will work, too.

Trotline Baits

Everything from Ivory soap to dead ground squirrels has been used to catch catfish on trotlines; however, some baits are better than others. Soft baits like congealed blood or chicken livers are effective, but often cats will pick the hooks clean without hooking themselves. Most trotline anglers prefer a tougher bait that is not easily pulled off the hook. They favor cut bait from bluegill, carp, suckers, herring or shad.

Live baits like bluegills, creek chubs or sucker minnows produce well for anglers. Live bait stays hardy and lives long after being impaled on a hook. If the water body you are trotlining has a

Complete Angler's Library

large flathead population, live baits will undoubtedly be the best all-around choice.

Many anglers regard catalpa worms as one of the finest catfish baits. These black-and-yellow larval caterpillars exude a smell that cats find irresistible. Many trotliners catch cats on bare hooks that were previously baited with catalpa worms. Collect these worms when available and freeze them for use later in the year. Nightcrawlers and whole crayfish, or the peeled-out tail sections, are top baits, as well.

Catfish trotlining is a wonderful way to spend a lazy summer's night. And, after seeing the monsters that the technique so often produces, your bass buddies just might forgive you for it!

Limblining Fun

Some American catfishing experts consider a twig bouncing over the water an adrenalin-surging, heart-quickening sign of sure success. These anglers use nothing more than a short piece of twine, a steel hook and a live bait. This combination could be the most formidable weapon ever conceived in the war against the whiskerfaces.

Some call them limblines. Others call them bush-hooks or throwlines. Whatever the name, limblines produce effectively.

Frank Billiter, a night-catfishing phenom, says, "The only technique in the world that will even come close to the productivity of bush-hooks is graveling (catching spawning cats by hand). When compared to trotlines ... well, there is no comparison. Bush-hooks provide more hook and bait control; you can position the bait exactly where the catfish feed, and you can position it in such a way that they are almost always hooked when they take the bait. And, once hooked, the fish rarely pull off of the line. And, it's a lot more fun than trotlining. You don't know if you have a fish on a trotline until you pull it out of the water. But, with a bush-hook, you can see that twig dancing from a hundred yards ... and you know there's a fish waiting for you!"

The Basic Bush-Hook

Limblining's basic rig consists of nothing more than a strong, quality hook tied to a 4- to 6-foot piece of strong, nylon twine. A wide-gapped 2/0 hook with a large eye works best for this task, and No. 15 bonded nylon line (approximately 100-pound test) will

When you see the limb dancing in the distance, you know you have a nice catfish waiting for you. Many anglers consider limblining more fun than trotlining because it's easier to tell if you have a fish.

not unravel like normal nylon twines. Bait the hook and tie the line to a small, green limb overhanging the water. Position the bait near the water surface. The hapless baitfish struggling near the water's surface attracts the catfish's attention.

Most anglers position their baits within a foot or so of the surface. Others, however, prefer to let the bait ride directly on the surface. "We tie the rig so that the bait is just barely under the surface," says Billiter. "I mean it's so close to the surface that the eye of the hook is often sticking up out of the water."

The twig you tie to your limbline should be alive, green, small and supple; it should bend and give as the fighting cat struggles. With a stout limb, you may find a broken line, broken limb or straightened hook come sunrise. It does not have to be a large branch; a small, green stick with a lot of give will hold a giant catfish. Long branches, however, are preferred. Often, a short branch will simply tear away from the tree.

Some anglers believe certain trees produce better than others. For example, many prefer willows and catalpa trees, probably because willow flies and catalpa worms naturally attract feeding cats. Some tree limbs, like boxwoods, are too brittle to hold a big fish.

Always measure the line before tying it to the tree limb. Make sure the line is short enough so the hook cannot reach the bank or some obvious snag or structure in the water. If the catfish can get to the shoreline or something solid in the water, it could tangle the line or snag the hook and pull free.

Bush-Hooks: When And Where

Most experts agree the best time for running limblines is during late spring and early summer when cats prepare to spawn. Generally speaking, the cats relate better to shallower water just before the spawn than they do at any other time. The immediate post-spawn period is a good bet, too. Nevertheless, cats can be taken on bush-hooks throughout the spring, summer and fall. And, if you happen to live in the southern United States, where temperatures remain moderate throughout the winter, limblining can be a four-season sport.

Anglers have learned to look for the largest cat populations in the deeper river holes and the dark impoundment depths. Limblining, however, focuses on shallow water. It is keyed to the catfish's nocturnal feeding migrations into the shallows adjacent to deeper water. Because more forage abounds in the shallows than in deeper pools, catfish move into these shallow-water areas. "When we set bush-hooks down a length of riverbank," says Frank Billiter, "we'll catch four times as many fish from shallow water as we will from the deeper pools. For one thing, I don't really believe that a baitfish struggling on the surface 15 feet or more above the catfish will attract much attention—it's just too far away. We always set our bush-hooks in water less than 10 feet deep."

Limblining works best in small- to mid-sized rivers and in an impoundment's headwaters. These areas clearly define the shoal-pool-flat structure, allowing the angler to position his baits in areas frequented by feeding cats. Also, the relatively shallow average depth means less distance between the bait and the catfish which increases your odds for success.

Because catfish swim into the current and move upstream when foraging, the best limbline locations center around the forward sections of deeper water pools. Bush-hooksets around shoals also produce, while sets along a long river flat often go unnoticed.

Different shoreline structure will offer different fishing results. Steep, near-vertical banks will produce more than shallow, gradually sloping, near-horizontal ones. Rocky banks, particularly those with bluff-type walls and large rocks, can be a superb hunting ground. Wooden snags hold flatheads, so keep your eyes peeled when scouting. Also, look for undercut banks, hollow logs, and tributaries entering the water body just upstream from a deeper hole.

And, without question, limblining works best after the sun has gone down.

Bush-Hooked Baits

Traditionally, anglers bait limblines with live fish. The baitfish's surface struggle attracts voracious cats. Frank Billiter says, "We don't bait our bush hooks with anything but freshly caught, live bait. Our favorite bait for catching a bunch of eating-sized cats is a 2- to 3-inch chub minnow. When we're hunting big cats, we prefer 6- to 8-inch chubs, suckers or even small catfish. Cats are cannibalistic, so smaller cats and mud-toms are a great bait."

Silver-dollar-sized bluegills work great on a limbline. These strong, hardy little fish swim on the surface for hours on end until

Limblines are one of catfishing's most effective, yet overlooked tools. This cat was one of several in the 3- to 6-pound range caught by this angler one evening.

Absentee Catfishing

Limblining anglers often use live bait, including large minnows, carp, small catfish and, where legal, bluegills. Bluegills are hardy baitfish that attract cats from considerable distances.

something big and ugly makes a meal of it. If you set your sights on a big, bruiser cat, try an 8- to 12-inch sucker or creek minnow, a hand-sized bluegill or a 6- to 8-inch carp. More substantial baits create more surface commotion, helping attract a larger cat's attention.

Trotlines, Limblines, Conservation And The Law

Trotlining and limblining is legal in most states. However, most restrict the number of hooks used on a trotline, as well as the trotline's length. Some states place restrictions on the trotline's construction. And, many states limit the number of limblines used by any one angler. To use a longer trotline or one equipped with more hooks, you may have to obtain a commercial fishing license from your state's department of fish and wildlife. Also, many states require that each limbline and trotline be labeled with your name, address and phone number. Familiarize yourself with your state's game and fish laws before partaking of trotline or limblining fun.

Check your trotlines and limblines each day, then remove them from the water when they will not be used for a period of time. It wastes our natural resources to allow catfish to die and spoil when using these absentee catfishing techniques. Check your hooks and lines at least once a day.

A baitfish struggling on the water's surface attracts most gamefish like a cast-iron triangle's ring attracts a hungry cowpoke. As a result, anglers take fish other than catfish on limblines, especially largemouths. Most states prohibit taking gamefish with methods other than rod and reel. That's why the NAFC encourages you to keep trying different baits if the ones you are using tempt too many other fish.

18

Plastic Jugs, 'Clined Cats

Throughout the year, thoughtless citizens dump trash into the feeder streams. This trash floats downstream, often covering acres of the water's surface; plastic jugs can be seen best. Bass anglers continue to swap a long-standing joke about the jugs: "The fish were on Clorox jugs today. Caught a few off of Prestone bottles, but the Bordon's milk jugs didn't hold a single one."

As humorous as that may (or may not) be, jugs do have a place in the sportfishing world. One of the easiest and most productive tactics known to catfishermen across the country involves drifting a bait under a plastic jug. And, while that technique works during much of the calendar year, it especially produces in a thermally stratified water body.

Summer Stratification

Thermal stratification needs to be dealt with on an annual basis in many ponds, lakes and reservoirs across the country. Basically, in the hot summer months, a vague water layer called the thermocline dictates the lowest depth at which cats feed, or even survive, in our impoundments. Thus, knowing the thermocline and the thermal stratification process will help the catfish angler catch more cats.

As the water's temperature changes, so does its density. Because cold water is heavier than warm water, it sinks beneath warmer water. Thus, a lake separates into layers of decreasing wa-

Find a jug, and you'll most likely find a cat. Jug fishing is a convenient way of catching cats because you just set the jugs out and come back later to find your fish.

Plastic Jugs, 'Clined Cats

Thermal Stratification

The thermocline in this illustration is represented by a darker gray band through the middle of the pond. In this case, it hasn't set in yet so there is still sufficient oxygen in the water throughout the depths to support catfish activity.

ter temperature during extended hot-weather periods.

In most ponds and lakes that lack distinct, relatively strong currents, a three-layered, thermal stratification of the water occurs. The top layer, the epilimnion, circulates as a result of the wind and wave action and remains well-oxygenated throughout the summer. In lakes that stratify, most aquatic life-forms, from fish to phytoplankton, live in this upper layer.

Scientifically, the thermocline is the band of water depth where water temperature decreases at a rate of .548 degrees (Fahrenheit) per foot. In most larger impoundments, the thermocline will begin some 15 to 25 feet below the surface. In smaller ponds, however, the thermocline may actually be found at a rather shallow depth of 5 or 6 feet.

In all stratified lakes, the cold water layer under the thermocline, called the hypolimnion, has a lower dissolved-oxygen level than the upper layers. In many lakes, the hypolimnion becomes uninhabitable because of the low oxygen content. This layer's dissolved-oxygen level also decreases as the season progresses. Therefore, although catfish can be found in the hypolimnion soon after stratification, they will, most likely, have vacated it by late summer.

In essence, this means that, in a thermally stratified water body, catfish anglers cannot simply cast their lines to the lake's bottom and expect to catch cats.

Locating The Thermocline

Knowing the thermocline's depth tells catfish anglers the maximum depth at which catfish will hold and feed. Using a depthfinder is one of the easiest ways of identifying this layer. Cranking up the sensitivity of a liquid crystal unit or paper graph while sitting over a deep portion of the lake usually reveals the location of the thermocline. Most often, the sensitivity will have to be increased to the halfway point (or higher) before the thermocline becomes visible. On a liquid crystal unit, it will appear as a horizontal line across the unit. On a paper graph, it will appear as a gray, hazy, poorly defined band across the paper. (When locating the thermocline with a sonar unit, the device most often picks up a mud layer forming in the thermocline, rather than the actual thermocline itself. This mud layer consists of dead algae and plankton which sank until reaching a depth where they became neutrally buoyant and then suspend. Most often, this occurs within the thermocline.)

A temperature probe can also be used to locate the thermocline. Lowering the probe (suspended on a coaxial cable marked in 12-inch increments) one foot at a time, actually "maps" the thermocline. When the probe reaches the thermocline, the temperature begins dropping rapidly (about half a degree per foot of depth). When the probe goes below the thermocline, the temperature continues falling, but at a much slower rate.

Capitalizing On The 'Cline

Unfortunately, most anglers never realize their favorite catfishing pond or lake is stratified. Instead, they pass off a fishless day with a "guess they weren't biting" excuse. In reality, they were probably presenting their baits beneath the feeding cats. Thus, if cats are mysteriously absent, check to see if the lake has stratified since your last visit.

Discovering a stratified lake does not mean "poor catfishing." Actually, it gives you some valuable insights into catching fish. Most important, it reveals that you will catch the most catfish from a depth just over the thermocline.

Carl Lowrance, the founder of a major depthfinder manufacturing firm, has mastered the relationship between thermoclines and catfish. Today, more often than not, you can find him on the water, enjoying his freedom and chasing his beloved catfish.

"After the lake has stratified," Lowrance says, "you can simply ignore all of the water beneath the thermocline when you are fishing. It's just not suitable to support life. Also, you can consider the thermocline a physical structure—almost like a new bottom—because catfish will relate to the thermocline as if it were the bottom of the lake."

Catfish suspend on the thermocline's top, lying on it just as they would a lake's floor in a non-stratified impoundment. "I have seen acres and acres of catfish suspended right on top of the thermocline," he says. "You can see them on a depthfinder of any sort, and it is a breathtaking sight. People just don't realize how many catfish there are in our lakes."

Because catfish in a stratified impoundment suspend on the thermocline just as if it were a physical structure, many anglers have trouble locating and catching them. Catfish suspending just over the thermocline could be anywhere in the lake. Searching for them compares to searching for a contact lens in Lake Erie. Lowrance, however, has developed a jug-fishing tactic tailor-made for thermocline catfishing.

"Since the catfish are as apt to be suspended in the middle of the lake as they are around the shoreline," he says, "I wanted a technique that would allow me to cover a lot of water pretty easily, and jug-fishing seemed to be a pretty good idea."

Jugs O' Plenty

Catfishing jugs can be made from virtually any plastic container. Anglers consider the jug size most important. Many think a small jug (like a quart oil bottle) would be too small to wear down a big cat. That may be true if you hook a monstrous cat, but an oil bottle will eventually tire a cat in the 15- to 30-pound range. The jug hunt may turn into a game of cat and mouse when the big cat pulls the jug underwater for several minutes, reemerging 100 feet away. When the jug performs its task, catfish will eventually end up resting on the bottom in the shallows along the shoreline. However, a large cat may be able to pull a small jug underwater far or long enough to hang up the line in a snag. Smaller jugs also become quite difficult to see over a giant expanse of water.

Large jugs like gallon-sized milk jugs or antifreeze containers work very well; so do 2-liter pop bottles. But, they will quickly fill your boat. Also, empty jugs blow out of fast-moving boats. Big jugs, however, can easily be seen across the lake and will quickly tire a hefty cat.

Whatever type of jug you use, be sure to carry enough with you. Fifteen to 20 jugs per angler makes for an entertaining evening. Any more and the play turns into work. Some states limit the number of jugs allowed per angler, and most require that anglers mark each jug with a name, address and phone number.

Plastic, quart-sized oil bottles work best when jugging in ponds and small- to mid-sized lakes. To modify a bottle, simply drill a small hole through the lid and run a piece of nylon cord through the hole. Next, select a metal washer that will fit into the bottle's spout and tie it to the line extending inside the lid. Drop the washer into the bottle, screw on the lid and tie a hook and sinker onto the line's terminal end.

In larger lakes and impoundments, you may want a larger jug that can be seen at a great distance. Two-liter pop bottles work well. Most have a lip molded around the neck allowing you to tie your line around the bottle's neck. Because most pop bottles have a clear-plastic exterior, paint them before using to increase visibility. Believe it or not, white jugs are perhaps the most visible across a large expanse of water. Yellow or fluorescent orange can also be easily spotted. When using milk jugs (be sure to use those with screw-on tops) and antifreeze bottles, tie your line to their molded handles.

The line length attached to each jug should be measured and recorded on the jug. This allows you to quickly determine the depth where most cats feed; thus, allowing you to adjust your

Commercial floats are available for jug fishing, but most anglers make their own out of plastic jugs or containers. This angler is setting out a commercial "jug."

other jugs accordingly. In ponds and small lakes that have a more shallow thermocline, 5 to 12 feet of line will usually be sufficient. In larger lakes, where the thermocline often develops 15 to 25 feet below the surface, you need longer lines. A sinker of ½ to 2 ounces should be tied to the line about 18 to 24 inches above the hook. Live baits and longer lines require heavier sinkers than do short lines and cut bait. In general, a 1/0, 2/0 or 3/0 hook will work for most chores.

For his catfishing jugs, Lowrance uses the same marker buoys commonly used by bass anglers. Although rather small and often hard to locate from a distance, these marker buoys offer the advantage of quick-and-easy depth adjustment with a simple half-hitch thrown around the buoy. Lowrance ties a 2-ounce sinker to his line's end, then attaches three 1/0 hooks on 12-inch leaders at

Complete Angler's Library

18-inch intervals from the cord's terminal end.

As a general rule, Lowrance ties his jug lines so the bait suspends 13 to 15 feet deep. "The thermocline might be deeper than that," he says, "but the catfish are always swimming upward to feed on shad. (Blue cats are notorious for feeding throughout the depths, and even up to the surface.) I've tried it with shallower and deeper sets, but I always have the most success with a rig set 13 to 15 feet deep."

Jugs can be baited with virtually anything, live or dead, but some offerings produce better than others. Live baits such as creek chubs and bluegill will live seemingly forever on a hook, even in warm water. Also, a live bait's struggles attract the cat's attention. Lowrance says his favorite offering, a big, 5- to 6-inch waterdog, is about four times as effective as a bluegill or a minnow. "When using both waterdogs and minnows," he says, "I'll catch four or five cats on the 'dogs to every one I catch on minnows." Cut bait from shad, herring, bluegill or even carp produces well. Soft baits like chicken liver, congealed blood and most stinkbaits do not work well when jugging because little cats pick the hooks clean before larger cats find the bait.

Jug-Fishing Basics

Jug-fishing involves more than dropping your baited jugs overboard, then finding them again sometime later. Jugging occurs mostly at night for many reasons. First of all, catfish are basically nocturnal creatures. Secondly, jugs pose a hazard to water skiers and boating traffic. Also, during the day, gar will often pick your baited hooks clean.

Some anglers prefer dropping their jugs, then checking them from time to time throughout the night. The game becomes angling's version of hide-and-seek, and provides a full night's entertainment for those who have insomnia. Other anglers prefer dropping their jugs at sundown, then checking them early the next morning. However, this method limits the number of fish that may be taken.

Wind plays a vital role in jug-fishing because it moves your jugs. If you drop the baited rigs on the lake's upwind side, the wind will carry the jugs across the water. Selecting the lake's widest span will allow you to cover the most water with the least effort, although you may have to be persistent because you may have

Often nice cats like this channel cat will be taken on jugs set in just a foot or two of water. Note that there is only about 2 feet of line on the jug in this picture.

some trouble locating your jugs when you decide to call it quits.

If you decide to retrieve your jugs at night, a powerful, hand-held spotlight is necessary. If you pick them up during the day, try searching for the jugs with the sun to your back. This eliminates glare, increases visibility and makes the jugs a bit easier to find.

"When you pick up a jug, hold it gently to see if there is a fish on it," says Lowrance. "If so, retrieve it gently, hand-over-hand while using your fingers as a make-shift drag. Many times, the fish will just barely be hooked, and the hook will tear free if you try to horse them in."

He also recommends examining the hook wound in each fish. "If the wound is bloodshot, it's an old wound and the fish has been on the jug for a long time," he says. "But, if the wound is clean, that tells you that the wound is new, and it might be worth your while to bait up a few more jugs and release them. Catfish seem to have definite feeding patterns, and you don't want to pass up a primary feeding period."

When you're done jugging for the day, be sure to retrieve all your jugs and take them home. If you do not want to save them for later use, dispose of them properly.

The Fall Turnover

When the air begins to cool in early autumn, the epilimnion (upper layer of the lake) has subsequently cooled. When the epilimnion temperature reaches the colder hypolimnion temperature, the layers will begin mixing and renew the oxygen levels while distributing nutrients throughout the lake. Autumn storms and heavy winds help speed the process which, in time, rejuvenates the lake. This is known as the fall "turnover," and when it occurs, catfish will again be found at all lake depths.

When the turnover occurs, the catfish environment changes drastically. Temperatures swirl and change, the pH varies, and the water turns a muddy brown color and exudes a sulfurous, swamp gas odor. For a few days, the catfish do not eat. But, because cats can cope with dramatic changes in their environment, they adapt quickly and resume feeding and stable holding patterns faster than the other gamefish.

Once the turnover is completed and the cats settle into routine patterns, many will have moved to deeper water holes. Jugging becomes a far less productive tactic than it was just two weeks

Fall Turnover

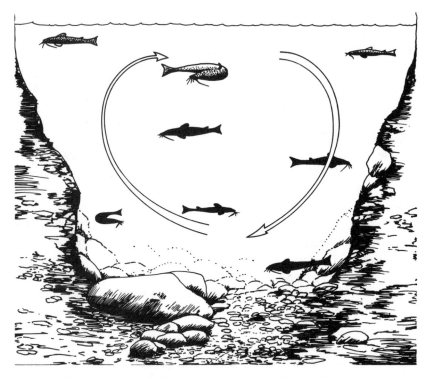

The arrows indicate the turnover of water that occurs in the fall when the surface water cools more quickly than the deeper water. Again, oxygen is well distributed throughout the depths.

ago. Smaller fish will still be found in the shallows for a short time, but the larger brutes haunt the lake or pond's deeper regions. For the most part, they will remain there through the winter's chill.

The Diversity Of Jugging

Although jug-fishing works best during the summer stratification of a flat-water pond or lake, it should not be limited to that single event. Jugging also works in the immediate pre- and post-spawn periods when cats haunt the lake's shallows. And, during the spawn itself, jugs released along shallow, rocky banks—riprapped banks are your best bet—will produce cats in both rivers and impoundments.

In small to mid-sized rivers, where the shoal-pool-flat sequence is evident, jugging is a superb tactic for those anglers equipped with a small boat. Because cats hold and feed in pools below shoals and, also, because blue cats often feed in the shoal's swift-water chutes, jugs drifted through the shoal and over the top of the pool naturally present a bait to the feeding cats. Most often, anglers anchor just upstream from the shoal and release a series of jugs into the current. The current carries the jugs through the shoal and into the pool below. Shortly thereafter, the anglers pick up anchor and chase the jugs. This sequence repeats two or three times at each shoal before moving to the next one.

Once you start jugging, you will be hooked for life. It is a simple method, one that will catch fish for you while you sleep. Kind of a catfish-o-matic!

19

Hands-On Catfishing

Passed down from father to son for generations, noodling has been a family affair practiced most often in the deep South. In essence, this remarkably sporting technique pits one angler against one fish, and the cat has the home-field advantage. Depending upon where you call home, noodling goes by many names: tickling, hogging, hand-grabbing, grappling and graveling. Noodling involves nothing more than wading in leech-infested waters and sticking your hand in deep, dark holes with the hopes that a giant catfish will mistake it for a small rodent. Then, when the whiskered demon sucks your hand into its gaping maw, you grab the fish's gill plate and wrestle the monster to the surface before he can drag you into the hole. Sounds like fun, huh?

The Vulnerability Of The Spawn

Noodling capitalizes on what may very well be the catfish's only weakness. In late spring, when the females grow fat with eggs and the males get that amorous glint in their eye, they begin searching for suitable spawning areas. This site selection and nesting process most often occurs after the water temperature has risen into the 70-degree range. This spawning season also spells trouble for many rod-and-reel anglers because, when the cats hole-up, it is difficult to get a bait to them.

All of America's larger cats—blues, channels, flatheads and whites—spawn in the same basic manner. First, a cavity, prefer-

Without a doubt, the most unusual method for catching fish is noodling. This angler has just successfully pulled a cat from its nest and to the surface. It pays to have buddies nearby to assist.

Hands-On Catfishing

ably one with a single opening, is selected and then prepared. Hollow logs, empty cans and drums, undercut banks, natural cavities in rocky bluffs, old muskrat holes, crevices in chunk rock and riprap, and even old appliances serve as adequate nesting sites. Seclusion and semi-darkness seem to be the major factors in nest selection.

Initially, the male moves into the cavity and begins sweeping it with his fins to enlarge the hole, removing any accumulated silt and creating a slick, hard-packed spawning surface. Shortly thereafter, the female moves into the hole and the actual egg-laying and fertilization process begins.

Catfish are superb guardians of their nests and wonderful parents to their young. Anything approaching the hole's entrance will be bitten, eaten or driven away. In most instances, however, the female cat will either leave the nest or be driven from it by the male soon after the egg-laying. The male, then, assumes the role as guardian.

The catfish's magnificent parenting leaves them susceptible to the noodling technique. Because the cats spawn in predictable, rather easily located holes, they become readily accessible to anglers. And, because spawning catfish try to engulf virtually anything that approaches their lair, they are, like a glass-jawed boxer, vulnerable to a well-placed fist.

Hunting The Holes

The Billiter family, a family of anglers from Pikeville, Kentucky, specializes in catfishing with rather unorthodox ways. And, noodling is one of their favorite tactics. Frank Sr. taught his sons, Frank Jr., Stacy, and Roy, the technique over a decade ago. Now, Frank Jr. teaches his son, Frank III, while Stacy instructs his son, Ryan.

Locating spawning holes can be very tedious. Given the number of catfish that swim in most of the waters across America, finding spawning holes is not truly difficult. Locating big-cat spawning holes, however, can be more time consuming.

"Most of the holes we find are in 2 to 6½ feet of water," says Frank Billiter Jr. "Current seems to play a role in the catfish's nest selection because we always find the most holes near creeks entering a river, along shoals and swiftly moving waters and in lake headwaters." Conversely, flat, still water rarely produces cats for

This pair of anglers is searching the submerged portion of the river bank for holes where catfish are nesting. If the hole is only partially submerged or the entrance slants upward, avoid it.

the Billiter family to haul in with their bare hands.

When noodling, the Billiters wade around the shoreline exploring hiding places with their hands. "Hollow logs will almost always hold a fish or two," Billiter says. "And, the washed-out depressions underneath large rocks are one of our finest spots for big cats.

"Before you ever stick your hand in a hole, you can usually tell if a cat is in there. If the entrance is soft and muddy, there won't be a fish in it. But, if it is hard and glassy-smooth, you can bet there's a cat waiting for you in the hole," says Billiter. You can normally judge the cat's size from the size of the hole's entrance; the larger the hole, the larger the cat. Oftentimes, however, cats will push gravel or sand into the entrance, almost as if they are trying to seal themselves in. "We have found entrances to holes anywhere from the size of a baseball to the size of a half-bushel washtub," Billiter says.

The most difficult task for the neophyte noodler is simply gaining the courage to stick his hand in a hole which another living creature, and a wild one at that, claims as its own. Once overcoming that fear, the catfish await. "Really, there's not much to it," says Billiter. "Once you find a hole, you just stick your fist into it and the fish will respond. Every catfish in a nesting hole, no matter how small or how big, will try to bite your hand when you stick it in the hole. A big cat will suck your hand into its mouth, but a small one will just peck at you." In either case, the experience definitely rates a 10 on the thrill-o-meter! What happens next depends upon the catfish's size. In the case of a small cat, say anything under 10 pounds, Billiter recommends trying to pin the catfish to the hole's bottom and then grabbing it over the head. This helps you gain a firm handhold around its spines.

"When a big cat takes my hand in its mouth," Billiter says, "I'll push the fish down against the bottom of the hole and then try to grab its lower jaw. A catfish's lower jaw is built just like a suitcase handle, and once you get hold of that handle you've pretty much got the cat licked."

The next step is pulling the fish toward you until only the head protrudes from the hole. Then, using your free hand, grab one of the cat's gill plates and pull it outward. This gives you a good hold on the fish, but also seems to freeze the fish so that it won't struggle too much.

Obviously, a terrific tug-of-war ensues. Try getting the fish to the surface before you run out of breath. "If the fish is a really big one, over 40 pounds or so, I'll try to yell at someone—if I'm not underwater—to get down in the water with me," Billiter says. "Then, each of us will get one hand on the cat's lower jaw and the other on each gillplate and together we'll pull him out. Going at it alone, a 40-pound cat will give you all the trouble you want, but it's a snap with two people."

Because they have such an enormous mouth, and because they are simply downright ferocious to begin with, flatheads could be considered the easiest cats to catch with your bare hands. It does not take much to get a large flathead to snatch your entire hand into its maw. Blues and channels, however, are a different story. Unless they are of hefty sizes, it can be difficult getting your

Complete Angler's Library

Larger catfish can be more of a battle than a man may want. Having a partner to help handle the cat, especially if you're doing it underwater, can be a real help.

hand into their mouth. Miss the first time and you probably will not get a second chance.

Tricks Of The Trade

In several states, noodlers sink their own nesting boxes for the cats. Typically constructed out of oak or cypress boards, the boxes usually measure approximately 4 feet in length, 2 to 3 feet in width, and 12 to 18 inches in height. First, assemble a solid box, then cut its opening. Using a circular saw, cut a 6- by 12-inch section from both the box's top and front, creating one large opening for the prospective tenant to use.

The boxes can be sunk in depths ranging from just a couple of feet to as deep as 20 to 30 feet, although scuba gear may be required to reach these deep-set boxes. To position the boxes and

Hands-On Catfishing

hold them in place, noodlers typically spread a thick layer of sand, gravel or mud in the box's bottom. Obviously, the position of each box should be accurately marked or recorded for future reference. These artificial nesting boxes are most beneficial in streams lacking an abundance of cover and structure. Channeled streams seem the best place to use them.

"The color yellow is an agitating influence to virtually every living animal in the world," says Dr. Loren Hill, a professor of zoology and director of the Oklahoma University Biological Research Center in Norman. "If you don't like the idea of poking your hand back in a hole when trying to find catfish, you can wear a bright yellow rubber glove and simply hold that gloved hand in front of the hole. Leave it there a few moments and if a cat is in the hole, it will most often strike at the glove."

Often, a noodler will find a hole that is rather deep from the entrance to the back. When the fish nest in the back of the hole, they will most often be out of reach. In this instance, noodlers increase their reach using a large treble hook attached to a handle or a short pole that increases their reach. The cats bite the hook as readily as they will a hand, and then the real fun begins! Although some noodlers do so, it is unwise to tether the pole to your wrist. Should the hook become snagged, you may run out of time (and air as well) before you can free yourself.

The Dangers Of Tickling

Noodling can be one of angling's most hazardous tactics. Most neophytes fear the catfish's dorsal-fin and pectoral-fin spines. In reality, however, these pose a very minor hazard, except with the smaller cats. Although these spines are needle-sharp in young catfish, they grow dull and become blunted as the catfish ages. A big cat's spines are no more sharp than a pencil eraser. In fact, noodlers often use them as a handhold on the cat when they have missed the lower jaw or the gillplate.

Being bitten by some other creature can happen with little warning. Snapping turtles can actually crush a finger, and the bite of a big loggerhead turtle is wicked. Muskrats (river rats) can turn a hand into hamburger in a split second. And, shorelines in many areas hold a lot of snakes.

To avoid these hazards, do not stick your hand in a hole that is not completely submerged. These creatures breathe air and sel-

Catfish come equipped with a good gripping spot on their lower jaw. The jaw is shaped some-what like a suitcase handle so the noodler need only get a grip on it and hang on.

Hands-On Catfishing   225

dom enter a hole that is not at least partially above the waterline. Muskrats sometimes build their lairs with the entrance hole under the water, then angle the tunnel upward and create a hollowed-out den above the waterline. If you find a hole that slopes upward, avoid it. Catfish rarely use them, but muskrats often do. And, when muskrats abandon their holes, other critters often assume their mortgages.

The greatest danger in noodling involves being trapped underwater or injuring yourself and losing consciousness. Hit your head while you are crawling under a rock just a few feet under the water and you will soon be crayfish fodder. If you feel compelled to dive, get yourself some scuba gear. Even though cumbersome, it may just save your life. And, never, ever go noodling alone. Take a partner or two.

The catfish themselves pose very little threat to a noodler. Granted, their sandpaper-like teeth rub your arm as raw as a piece of chopped steak, but they will not do any real damage. Some noodlers wear long, heavy rubber gloves with the fingers cut off just to protect the skin on their wrists and forearms. You may bleed a bit, and your arms might be sore the next day, but you will eventually heal.

Noodling: The Law And Conservation

Because noodling takes advantage of the catfish's spawning habits, the best time to do it roughly coincides with the cat's spawning season. Many states, in fact, have set noodling seasons. In Mississippi, for example, the season runs from May 1 through July 15. Just a bit farther north in Kentucky, where waters warm a bit later and the catfish's spawn is later, the noodling season runs from June 10 through August 31. In those states with set hand-fishing seasons, noodling at any other time is poaching. Get caught and you may lose your boat, a lot of money and several nights' sleep in your own bed. Also, some states mandate that noodling only be done during daylight hours.

How does hand-grabbing affect the catfish population? Donald C. Jackson, Ph.D., an associate professor at the Mississippi State University Department of Wildlife and Fisheries, leads an extensive, on-going research study that will, it is hoped, answer that question. However, no definite conclusions have yet been reached. Nevertheless, Jackson sees a need for conserving our big

Gloves are a good choice for noodlers because they not only improve the grip but offer protection from the catfish's sandpaper-like teeth that can rub your skin raw.

cats. "They are the largest predators," he says, "and the top of the food chain in most of our freshwater lakes and rivers. For that reason alone, sportsmen should conserve our large cats, especially the flatheads because they are exclusively predatorial.

"People do not have to catch a lot of 40- to 80-pound catfish to have a good time," he continues. "Hand-grabbing is a great deal like hunting a trophy whitetail. Anglers are willing to put up with day after day after day of unsuccessful fishing for that one chance of battling a real trophy. And, just as deer hunters should not kill young bucks just to put meat on the table, noodlers should release the young flatheads and blues and keep a mess of smaller channel cats. Our giant catfish truly are a big-game animal, and we need to treat them as such."

John Burris, chief of the education and environmental section of Mississippi's Department of Wildlife Conservation, says, "We have no concrete data on the matter, and we won't until Dr. Jackson's study is completed. But, here in Mississippi, even though it is a traditional sport, noodling is not a very popular one. We have only a handful of anglers practicing the technique and, so far, we cannot see that it is hurting our catfish populations. If that is the case, we see no reason to ban the sport." (Noodling is illegal in some states, so check your game and fish laws before jumping into the water.)

Some states limit the number of catfish that may be taken when grappling. Kentucky law, for example, states, "The daily creel limit (when hand-grabbing) is 15 rough fish, no more than five of which can be catfish."

For the sake of the catfish fraternity as a whole, and for the catfish themselves, keep a big fish or two, keep a nice mess of channel cats, but release the smaller flatheads and blue cats that will one day grow to be those monsters that give scuba divers the "willies."

Catfish On The Rocks

Bob Holmes, a catfisherman extraordinaire from Trenton, Tennessee, has developed a remarkably effective rod-and-reel technique for catching spawning catfish. In essence, Holmes hunts those areas where cats should be in the spring: along the riprapped areas of bridges and marina harbors, broken rock banks and river bluffs with vertical rock walls harboring a maze of cracks, fissures and chunk rock (all of which are likely spawning grounds for the cats).

Holmes says that cats initially begin showing up on the rocks when the surface temperature moves into the low 60s. In his Kentucky Lake and Tennessee River stomping grounds, the spawning season begins in late April and extends through the month of May and on into June. "The best early-season fishing is usually found on banks that face south or southwest," he says, "because they are the first to warm up. Riprapped areas are good, too, because they warm quickly and then tend to hold the heat (thereby warming the surrounding waters)." Once productive spawning areas are located, anglers can return to them throughout the four to eight weeks of the spawn and continue to catch catfish.

"I fish primarily for eating-sized cats," Holmes says, "primarily

If the noodler can get the right grip on the catfish's lower jaw, it will tend to quiet the struggling fish, much like holding the lower jaw of a bass.

those in the 2- to 5-pound range. There's a lot more of them and they are easy to catch so, in addition to stocking my freezer, this technique is a lot of fun to boot!"

Holmes matches his tackle to these smaller cats. "I like to use a very long rod, usually a heavy two-piece or telescopic crappie pole, because it provides exceptional line control." A quality, medium-action spinning reel spooled with 12-pound line attaches to the rod's reel seat. Holmes says a good spincast reel will serve that task almost as well. "This really is kind of a light rig for catfishing," he says, "but it works very well when you are targeting smaller cats. I do, however, always carry a few extra spools for the reel already rigged with line because, more often than not, I'll hook into a fish or two that will take every bit of my line and keep going!"

Noodling For Catfish

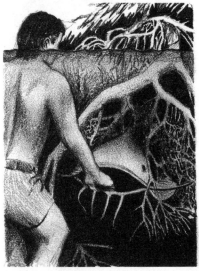

This drawing gives you a "below-the-surface" view of what happens when a noodler probes the entrance of a nest.

His terminal tackle rig consists of a 4- to 6-inch slip-cork that can slide on the line, enough weight (placed on the line 4 to 6 inches above the hook) to make the cork stand up and sit rather low in the water, and a No. 6 or No. 4 treble hook tied to the line's terminal end. "I use a bobber-stop to control the depth of my bait," Holmes says. "This allows me to change the depth without having to retie the rig."

Bobber stops also facilitate casting by reducing the amount of line dangling from the rodtip. The bobber-stop fits to the line at the desired depth and then is reeled through the rod's line guides while the bobber slides down to the sinker. After the cast, the sinker pulls the line through the slip-cork until the bobber-stop meets the cork.

This technique should be used in shallow water. Holmes most often begins his search for the spawning cats with a bait dangling about 3 feet below the surface. "It is kind of a flip and pitch tactic," he says. "I like to position my boat with the bow pointed into the wind or current, parallel to the bank and overtop of the depth I want to cover. Then, I just pitch the bait forward and drift backward with the wind or current. If I don't have any luck with a bait at that depth, I'll scoot away from the bank just a bit and adjust the bobber-stop so the bait rides 5 to 6 feet under the surface." He repeats that sequence until the most productive depth has been discovered.

Over the years, Bob Holmes has developed a decided preference in his bait selection for taking these 2- to 5-pound cats. "I cut a nightcrawler into pieces and then drape one or two, 1- to 2-inch pieces over two of the hook points on the treble hook," he says. "On the third point, I'll use a piece of peeled shrimp about the size of the end of my finger. It is a small offering, but I have yet to find anything that the cats will hit as well."

How effective is this technique for catching spawning cats on the rocks? "Heck, I usually fill a cooler in an hour or two," Holmes says. "If you spend an entire morning fishing on the rocks when the cats are biting, you can probably catch a hundred pounds of fish with no trouble. I know a lot of fishermen who use this technique and, during the four- to six-week spawning period, they'll catch all the cats they want for the entire year!"

20

Caring For Your Catch

There is no disputing the fact that catfish are one of the finest tasting fish swimming in freshwater. (Or, in salt-water for that matter.) Catfish flesh is firm in texture, moist and quite flaky. Above all, it offers a superb yet mild flavor with very little "fishy" taste.

When compared to beef, chicken or pork, catfish is low in to-tal fat, saturated fat and cholesterol; thus, it is the perfect com-plement to the health-conscious diet. Medical studies have shown that reducing fat and cholesterol-intake reduces levels of serum cholesterol and the risk of heart attacks. Catfish is also high in protein, low in calories, low in sodium and a great source of vita-mins and minerals. It also contains some Omega-3 fatty acids, which many researchers have credited with reducing the risk of heart disease. But, best of all, it tastes good.

For the best possible flavor from your catfish, you must care for it properly after the catch. Virtually every instance of "bad" tast-ing catfish can be traced to improper handling or cleaning prac-tices, or an unskilled chef!

After The Fight
Ideally, catfish—make that all fish—that are earmarked for the skillet should be killed, gutted and placed on ice immediately after they are caught. Fish flesh is among the most perishable foods known to mankind and, believe it or not, it may begin to deteri-orate even before the fish dies. Fish kept on a stringer or in a warm

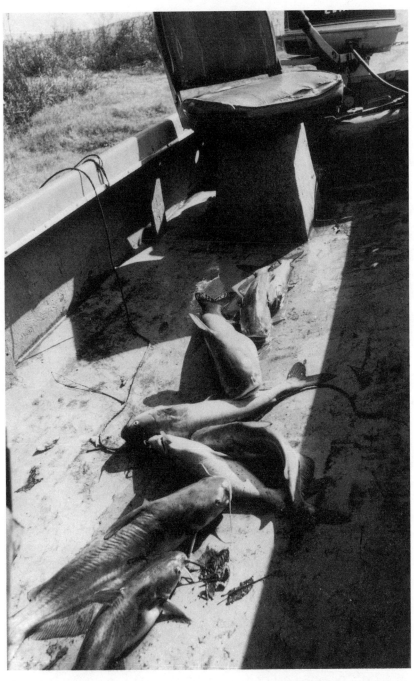

Your starting point in caring for your catch is after you have filleting-sized catfish like these. These were placed in the bottom of the boat, instead of a livewell, for photographic purposes.

Caring For Your Catch

A sharp filleting knife is always good, but some catfishermen have brought improved kitchen technology to the cleaning board by using electric knives.

livewell all day before being killed will simply not taste as good as properly harvested ones. And, when a fish dies, it deteriorates at an extremely rapid rate.

Bacterial invasion and the efficient digestive function inherent in all fish causes this rapid deterioration. To prevent bacterial growth in the flesh, gut the fish as quickly as possible, taking care not to spill any of the bacteria-rich stomach and intestinal fluids on the flesh. Then, wash the fish thoroughly in cold water to eliminate blood and bacteria, and place the fish on ice.

When a fish dies, its own cells actually begin to digest themselves. Enzymes located within the cells are responsible for this phenomenon, known as autolysis. This cell breakdown greatly reduces the flavor of fish, but can be retarded by simply cooling the fish immediately after it dies. Maintaining cell integrity in fish

Complete Angler's Library

flesh is vital in developing quality tablefare. When fish freeze, the cells rupture, thereby losing a great deal of texture and some flavor, as well. This is why fresh fish taste superior to frozen fish. When fish freeze, thaw and then freeze again, they will have a texture almost as soft as oatmeal when thawed again.

Take care of catfish after they are caught and you will be well rewarded at the dinnertable.

Cleaning Catfish

Various ways to clean catfish exist, but filleting and pan-dressing are the most commonly used techniques.

First, you will need a good fillet knife. One with a 7-inch blade works best. Sharpen it before each use and keep a crock-stick handy for touch-ups. A board of some kind, either a large cutting board or a leftover plank of some sort, should be used as the cleaning station. You will also need a pair of pliers for removing any skin missed in the cleaning process and for pulling fins out of pan-dressed fish.

A bowl full of ice water should be used for storing fish after cleaning until packaged. A teaspoon of salt added to this water will help pull any residual blood out of the fish.

Filleting

Fillets cook faster and more thoroughly than do pan-dressed catfish, and most people find that they taste better, as well. Granted, you will waste a small amount of meat, but the convenience is worth the cost.

Step 1: With the catfish lying on its side, make an angled cut from a point just behind the head down to a point just below the fish's midline. Cut down to the spine, but not through it. Next, insert the knife's point into the initial incision and cut through the fish's side all the way to the anus. If you have not gutted the fish, be careful not to puncture the gut.

Step 2: Insert the knife into the initial incision with the blade's cutting edge pointed toward the tail. Hold the head and slice the fish all the way to the tail, taking a slab of meat from the fish's side. Keep the blade parallel with and against the spine. You will be cutting through the rib bones, so expect some resistance. When cleaning larger cats, an electric fillet knife makes the job a lot easier.

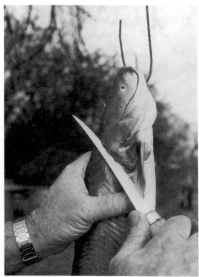

An Oklahoma catfisherman prefers to fillet his cats while they're hanging upright instead of laying on a cleaning board. The steps are the same as outlined by the author. Here, the length-wise slits around the dorsal fin are made (left) as well as the cuts behind the gill plate (right) in preparation for skinning.

Step 3: Either clamp or hold the fillet's tail-end with the skin-side down. Cut through the flesh down to the skin, but do not cut through the skin. Turn the knife toward the fillet's head-end and, with the blade angling slightly downward, separate the skin from the flesh by running the knife (using a cutting motion) between the two.

Step 4: Remove the rib bones and the row of smaller bones that are set at a right angle to the ribs by slicing through the fillet around the rib cage. To reduce the fillet's fat (and contaminant) content, remove a thin strip of meat from the fillet's lower (belly) side. Remove any of the red lateral line tissue that you may find.

Step 5: Rinse the fillet under running water and toss it into a pan of ice water. Repeat the process in removing the fillet on the other side of the catfish.

Pan-Dressing

This method, which works best on smaller cats, results in a nice piece of fish flesh ideal for baking or creating a "stuffed fish" dish. Although none of the flesh goes to waste, the bones are left intact and must be removed or picked around at the dinner table.

Complete Angler's Library

The skin is pulled off fairly easily when the cat is upright (left), and then the fillets are cut apart (right).

Step 1: Starting just behind the adipose fin, make a shallow cut just beneath the skin reaching all the way to the dorsal spine. Now, turn the blade downward and cut down to the spine (but not through it).

Step 2: Holding the body in one hand and the head in the other, bend the head downward to break the backbone. (On larger fish, you may have to cut through the backbone, but be careful not to cut into the abdominal cavity.)

Step 3: Insert your forefinger over the end of the spine and into the rib cage. Slowly pull the head downward, then toward the tail. (This will peel the head, skin and viscera (guts) free from the fish's fleshy portion.) If you desire, the tail, adipose fin and anal fin may be removed. To remove the anal fin, simply grab it at the lower rear with a pair of pliers and pull upward toward the fish's head. After rinsing the flesh in running water, it can be cooked or frozen.

Although large cats can be dressed in this manner, it takes a little more work and a lot more strength. Big cats are too large to cook whole. If you do not fillet them, consider pan-dressing them and then cutting them into steaks. Once dressed, the fish can be

Caring For Your Catch

The resulting fillet is then trimmed of adipose tissue which, as the author notes, contains possible contaminants. The trimmed fillet is ready for the pan or freezer.

sliced into steaks approximately 1-inch thick.

Reducing Fat And Contaminant Concentrations

Many of the contaminants that taint catfish flesh are naturally bound into the catfish's adipose (or fat) tissues. Removing these portions of the catfish not only reduces your possible intake of those contaminants, but reduces the fat content of the fish and helps to preserve its quality and taste when freezing. These fatty areas taste rather strong and will oxidize (or turn rancid) more quickly than the surrounding tissues.

Most of the catfish's adipose tissue is deposited in three areas of the body. The dorsal adipose is located along the fish's back, while the ventral adipose runs along the belly. The lateral adipose tissue follows the lateral line along both sides of the catfish. For a tastier, healthier meal, remove these areas when cleaning your cats. Filleting the fish will remove the largest portions of the dorsal and ventral adipose. The lateral adipose is typically scant to begin with, and goes along with the red lateral line tissue that should be sliced or scraped from a fillet. (This red tissue is obvious in flathead fillets, but not in blues, channels and whites.)

Complete Angler's Library

The fillets that have been rinsed in cold water are ready to be put in sealable plastic freezer bags. Make sure to label each bag by writing the contents and the date on the outside.

Caring For Your Catch

Storing Your Fish

The best tasting fish is cooked fresh. Granted, you may not be in the mood for a big meal after a long night on the water, but you can safely refrigerate your cleaned and dressed catfish for a day or two before using them.

The best method is storing them on ice. Crushed ice is better than chunks or cubes because it provides a more intimate contact between fish and ice. Simply layer the fish between blankets of crushed ice in a large bowl or plastic container. Cover the bowl with some type of clinging plastic wrap and place it in the coldest part of your refrigerator. Whenever you think about it, drain off any water and add more crushed ice. Do not allow the fish to sit in water any length of time.

Catfish can be frozen with very little flavor loss for several months, if done correctly. The two major culprits in decreasing the quality of frozen fish are dehydration and oxidation; however, the effects of both may be minimized through careful packaging of the fish.

Dehydration occurs when the fish loses moisture. Freezer burn may then occur, with the flesh turning an opaque, whitish color and leaving it with the texture of old boot leather. During oxidation, oxygen combines with the fats and oils in the fish flesh, eventually causing them to turn rancid and spoil. This taints the flavor of the entire fish.

When freezing fish, the goal is to seal in moisture and lock out oxygen. There are several ways to accomplish this task. First, choose a packaging material that is not porous. Cling wraps and thick, sturdy, plastic, sealable bags designed for freezer use are probably best.

To minimize waste, divide your catfish into meal-sized portions before freezing.

To freeze catfish for an extended time period, wrap the dressed flesh in a cling wrap, taking great care to force out any air between the fish and the plastic. Next, wrap it again in either another layer of cling-wrap plastic or a sheet of aluminum foil. For a bit of added protection, wrap it once more in freezer paper and label the finished product with the contents and date.

Another method works best with boneless fillets. Place the desired number of fillets in a plastic, sealable bag of the appropriate size. While bagging the fish, allow your sink to fill with clean wa-

Enough fillets for a meal are packed in individual bags (in this case, four to a package) from which the air has been squeezed out. Some pack the fillets in water to ensure that all the air has been removed.

ter. Next, submerge the fillet-filled bags under the water and force out any air. A small amount of water left in the bag is acceptable. Seal the bags underwater. Next, dry them, wrap them in freezer paper, label each with the date and contents and then place in the freezer.

Some anglers prefer to freeze their fish in water. Actually, the water does not serve any purpose other than helping to eliminate air pockets around the fish. Again, fillets work best for this method. Simply pack the fish tightly into an airtight plastic container with a snap-on lid. Pack the container with as much fish as possible, and try to eliminate any dead spaces between pieces. Fill the container with water and put the lid in place, allowing the excess water to flow out of the container. Using freezer tape, label the container with the contents and the date and then place them in the freezer.

When freezing fish, freeze it as quickly as possible. Place it in the coldest portion of the freezer until it is frozen rock-solid. If you place a lot of fish into your freezer at one time, be sure to turn the temperature control all the way down until the fish freezes.

When packaged properly and kept at zero (Fahrenheit) or be-

Catfish gourmets agree that nothing beats fried catfish. In this case, the fillets have been rolled in batter and then fried to a golden brown in a large frying pan.

low, most fish will retain flavor and texture for at least three months. Because catfish have a low-fat content, that period may be six months or so, especially if you removed all the adipose tissue. Unfortunately, the quality of fish meat unavoidably deteriorates the longer it is kept frozen.

For best results, thaw the fish in the refrigerator (although this may take at least 24 hours). If you need the fish a bit more quickly, leave it wrapped in its freezer packaging and place in a bowl of cold water. Fish should never be thawed at room temperature. This causes parts of the fish to deteriorate while other parts are still thawing.

Cooking With Catfish

Like most fish, catfish cook rather quickly. As a general rule, allow 10 minutes per inch of thickness (measured at thickest part of fish) when cooking at 425 to 450 degrees.

Catfish can be fried, smoked, blackened, broiled, baked, grilled, steamed, stewed or stir-fried with remarkable success. Catfish can be easily substituted in most recipes calling for a chicken breast. Make fish fingers, fish sticks or fish nuggets. Use leftover catfish in cold pasta salads. And, don't forget about America's favorite, fried catfish fillets and hush puppies. (Recipes for catfish dishes can be found in NAFC's annual fishing cookbook editions.)

Eat hearty, and enjoy!

Index

244

Tailraces, 180-191
Temperature probe, 210
Thermocline, 163-164, 170, 206-217
Threadfin shad, 113
Throwlines, 199
Topographic map, 171, 176
Transducer, 84-85
Trotlines, 10, 192-199
Tube lures, 122

U

Ultraviolet light, 93-94

V

V-hull boats, 105-106
Van Vactor, Darrell, 175-176
Ventral adipose, 238
Vertical structure, 171

Video sounders (depthfinders), 83-84

W

Water conditions, 53
Water depth, 201-202
Water pH, 53-54, 216
Water temperature, 28, 31-32, 52,
   163-164, 170, 206-217
Weberian Apparatus, 32, 42
Weedlines, 162
White catfish, 18, 24-25, 53
   anal fin, 24
   color, 24
   habitat, 24, 25
   range, 24
   weight, 24
Willow cats, 16